# The Supreme Court of the United States

# The Supreme Court of the United States

## Its Business, Purposes, and Performance

Paul A. Freund

*Meridian Books*
THE WORLD PUBLISHING COMPANY
*Cleveland and New York*

PAUL A. FREUND

Paul A. Freund was born in St. Louis, Missouri, on February 16, 1908. He took his LL.B. and S.J.D. degrees at Harvard and served as Justice Brandeis' law clerk in 1932-33. In 1939, after holding various government legal posts, Mr. Freund became Professor of Law at Harvard. Since 1958 he has been Carl M. Loeb University Professor there. Professor Freund is the author of *On Understanding the Supreme Court* (parts of which have been revised and incorporated in this book), and co-editor of *Constitutional Law: Cases and Other Problems*. He is a frequent contributor to legal periodicals.

*AN ORIGINAL MERIDIAN BOOK*

*Published by The World Publishing Company*
*2231 West 110th Street, Cleveland 2, Ohio*
*First printing August 1961*
*Second printing September 1962*

*Library of Congress Catalog Card Number: 61-15601*
*Printed in the United States of America* WP962

## CONTENTS

# PREFACE

The seven chapters of this volume are based on essays written at various times over the past dozen years. They endeavor to help toward an understanding of the Supreme Court by viewing it from several angles of vision: its business and its functions in American life; its canons and its performance in the central fields of civil liberties and the maintenance of the federal system; the qualities of mind that characterize a liberal judge on the Court; the role of counsel before it; and the criticisms recently leveled against it. While the chapters were composed independently, it is hoped that they are given a measure of unity by a pervading philosophic outlook.

Chapters II ("Concord and Discord"), V ("Portrait of a Liberal Judge: Mr. Justice Brandeis"), and VI ("Judge and Company") are largely taken from the three chapters of the author's book *On Understanding the Supreme Court* (Little, Brown and Company, 1949), now out of print. Chapter I ("The Business of the Court") appeared in the December 1951 number of the *Canadian Bar Review.* Chapter III ("Standards for Civil Liberties") was published in the April 1951 number of the *Vanderbilt Law Review.* Chapter IV ("Umpiring the Federal System") appeared in the *Columbia Law Review* for April 1954. Chapter VII ("The Court and Its Critics") is taken from an address published in the *New York State Bar Bulletin* for February 1959. The essays have been amplified where it seemed desirable to take account of further developments, and in a few places have been recast for greater clarity. To each of the publications mentioned grateful acknowledgment is made for permission to reprint.

*Harvard Law School* PAUL A. FREUND
*June 1961*

# The Supreme Court of the United States

# I. THE BUSINESS OF THE COURT

At the 1959 term the Supreme Court of the United States disposed of almost eighteen hundred cases. This bare and arresting figure suggests a number of inquiries. How do these cases reach the Court and what is the process of deliberation and adjudication by which they are translated from items on the docket to controversies disposed of? What are the significant functions of the Court and what are the standards that guide it in the discharge of those functions? What is the larger role of the Court in the symbolism, attachment to which forms the basis of a constitutional system? These questions may be conveniently subsumed under three heads: (1) The Jurisdiction and Administrative Side of the Court; (2) The Court as Arbiter; (3) the Court as Symbol.

## I. *The Jurisdiction and Administrative Side of the Court*

Article III of the Constitution of the United States provides that the judicial power of the United States "shall be vested in one supreme Court, and in such inferior Courts as the Congress may from time to time ordain and establish." The judges of all the federal courts hold office, by virtue of other provisions of Article III, during good behavior; they are appointed by the President with the advice and consent of the Senate, and their compensation may not be diminished during their continuance in office. While the bare existence of the Court is thus constitutionally secured, the size of the Court is left to Congressional legislation, as is the scope of its appellate jurisdiction. After setting forth the several classes of controversies over which the federal courts may be given jurisdiction, Article III states: "In all Cases affecting Ambassadors, other public Ministers and Consuls, and those in which a State shall be Party, the supreme Court shall have original Jurisdiction. In all the other Cases before mentioned, the supreme Court shall have appellate Jurisdiction, both as to Law and Fact, with such Exceptions, and under such Regulations as the Congress shall make."

Standing as it does at the apex of a hierarchy of state and federal courts, the Supreme Court is no ordinary court of last resort. Its special position does not fit easily into the well-worn epigram that trial courts search for truth and appellate courts search for error. Its contemporary province was marked out by the Judiciary Act of 1925, which in conception and drafting was largely the work of the Court itself under the aegis of Chief Justice Taft.

The philosophy of the 1925 act is that, on the whole, only controversies of general importance should find their way to the calendar of the Supreme Court of the United States. The technique for realizing this philosophy is the certiorari jurisdiction of the Court. One must recall that appellate cases may be taken to the Court by two routes, appeal and certiorari, depending on the nature of the case. The avenue of appeal, which replaced the older writ of error, is reserved principally for cases from state courts in which the highest court of the state has held a state statute valid under the federal Constitution. Other cases from the highest courts of the states—decisions holding state statutes unconstitutional, construing federal statutes, or involving federal privileges and immunities like full faith and credit to judgments of sister states—must take the avenue of certiorari. The functional difference between appeal and certiorari is that jurisdiction under the former is obligatory, under the latter discretionary with the Supreme Court.

The canons governing the Court's exercise of its discretion in granting or denying petitions for certiorari have been set out in the Supreme Court Rules. Chief among the factors that will move the Court to grant certiorari are the general importance and novelty of the issues in the case, the existence of a conflict of decisions among the intermediate federal courts of appeals, or an apparent departure by the court below from a controlling authority of the Supreme Court. It should be added that the privilege of self-determination granted to the Court in its certiorari jurisdiction by the Act of 1925 has in practice been carried over to some extent to the disposition of appeals. Just as petitions for certiorari are granted or dismissed on the moving papers (the petition and the respondent's brief in opposition), and only the granted cases are set down for briefs and argument on the merits, so in administering its cognate jurisdiction on appeal the Court requires a statement of jurisdiction by the appellant (to which the appellee may oppose a motion to dismiss or affirm), and on the basis of these papers an appeal may be dismissed without argument "for the want of a substantial federal question." Thus a constitutional decision of a state court which is technically entitled to review but which would raise no issues requiring a full submission on the merits will not be allowed a place on the calendar for argument.

Cases from the federal courts of appeals (of which there are ten, plus the Court of Appeals for the District of Columbia) typically reach the Supreme Court by certiorari. These intermediate federal courts are the appellate tribunals for the federal district courts, whose jurisdiction, partly concurrent with that of the state courts, extends to cases arising under the Constitution or federal laws and those between citizens of different states. In contrast to the review of state court decisions, where some constitutional or other federal question must have been the turning point in the judgment, the Supreme Court may review decisions of the federal courts of appeals on any issue, including a misapplication by the court of relevant state law.

In addition to the flow of cases from the state courts and the federal courts of appeals, there is a final group which reaches the Supreme Court on direct appeal from the federal district courts (of which there is at least one in every state). These rather exceptional opportunities for direct review are limited to cases in which a district court has held an act of Congress unconstitutional; or has dismissed an indictment on the ground of construction of the governing criminal statute; or has decided a civil suit brought by the government under the federal antitrust laws. In addition, direct appeal to the Supreme Court will lie from the decision of a specially constituted three-judge district court, which must be convened to hear applications for injunction against the enforcement of state or federal laws on the ground of unconstitutionality and to hear petitions to set aside certain orders of the Interstate Commerce Commission and a few kindred agencies.

Nothing has been said of the original, as distinguished

from the appellate, jurisdiction of the Supreme Court. In fact the original jurisdiction is narrowly confined and strictly construed. It extends principally to controversies between two or more states (in which the states must be the real parties in interest), between the United States and a state, and between a state and citizens of another state. An occasional dispute over boundaries or apportionment of interstate waters or the ownership of minerals in the marginal sea is filed in the Supreme Court and if a determination of facts is required, is referred to a special master for hearing and report.

With these dreary details of jurisdiction in mind, one can perhaps understand how the Court managed to dispose of almost eighteen hundred cases at the 1959 term. Actually less than fourteen per cent of the cases were decided on the merits, and less than seven per cent with opinions. The others were disposed of mainly by denial of petitions for certiorari.

While the device of statutory certiorari has enabled the Court to keep abreast of its docket and indeed to harry counsel into the argument of cases more rapidly after the grant of certiorari than counsel would sometimes choose, there is still some feeling within and without the Court that the opportunity for unhurried deliberation, full consultation, and scholarly opinion-writing is inadequate. The Court can, within limits, control the volume of cases to be argued and decided on the merits; it cannot control the volume of petitions for certiorari and appeal papers filed by counsel. In recent years there has been a swelling of applications for certiorari owing to the Court's growing concern with the due process requirements of criminal procedure in state and federal courts, combined with its liberal practice in receiving petitions *in forma pauperis.*[1] Such petitions of late have reached a total of around a thousand a term, and since ordinarily they reflect less careful technical skill in their preparation and are presented in typewritten rather than printed form, the burden on the Court's time may be even greater than the proportionate number of these petitions would suggest.

The Court normally sits to hear arguments during two-week periods followed by two or more weeks of recess, from October to June. Conferences are held on Friday and if necessary, on Saturday for the consideration of cases argued during that week and for action on certioraris ready for disposition. Unlike the practice in some of our state courts, opinions are assigned not by rotation but by the Chief Justice, or if he is in the minority, by the senior Associate Justice in the majority. As is evident to all readers of the *Supreme Court Reports*, the practice of framing dissenting opinions is freely indulged in, and of late years there has been a growing tendency to prepare special concurring opinions. Thus the practice stands midway between that of the seriatim opinions of the House of Lords and that of the unitary opinion of the Privy Council (lest, we are told, the Crown would be confused by conflicting advice).

Amid all the shifts of doctrine that have occurred in the more than a century and a half of the Court's life, one principle has been steadfastly professed: that the Court will decide only an actual case or controversy and will not render an advisory opinion or a judgment in a non-adversary proceeding.[2] This is the central paradox of the Court's jurisdiction and functions: its special role is to resolve questions of general importance transcending the interests of the litigants and yet it will do so only where necessary to adjudicate a conventional legal dispute between the parties. Faced with this paradox, it is not surprising that on occasion the Court has wavered in its fidelity to the principle of abstention. Occasionally the Court has been moved by the gravity of the issues and the pressures for settlement to pass upon constitutional questions in cases that seem to have been something less than bona fide adversary proceedings calling for the exercise of traditional judicial power.

The sorry consequences of certain of these departures have doubtless confirmed the Court in the wisdom of its professed canons of self-limitation. Looking back on the *Dred Scott* decision,[3] which by holding unconstitutional an act of Congress forbidding slavery in the territories, foreclosed one mode of compromise of the gathering tensions before the Civil War, it can be seen that the decision might have been avoided on the ground that the status of the Negro was to be determined by the law of Missouri, where the case arose. Looking back on the *Income Tax* cases[4] which held that a tax on income from property was a tax on the property itself and thus a direct tax which had to be apportioned according to population under the Constitution, it is evident that the decision could have been avoided by recognizing that there was no equity jurisdiction in the suit by a stockholder to enjoin his corporation from paying the tax, inasmuch as there was an adequate remedy at law by way of payment and claim for refund. It is noteworthy that these two instances were among the three that Charles Evans Hughes characterized as the principal self-inflicted wounds of the Court.[5] Noteworthy too is the fact that although in 1935 Congress enacted a Declaratory Judgments Act, the statute is limited to "cases of actual controversy" and the Supreme Court has been chary of permitting it to enlarge the standing of litigants to raise constitutional issues.

Back of the formal bases for the Court's self-denying ordinance—the requirement of "case" or "controversy" in Article III of the federal Constitution and the doctrine of separation of powers—lies the conviction that the framework of a traditional adversary proceeding furnishes a safeguard against premature or ill-advised decisions in the constitutional field. Especially is this true of issues of constitutionality which turn, as they increasingly do, on questions of fact and degree and application to persons and circumstances.

## II. *The Court as Arbiter*

The determination of common-law controversies forms a steadily diminishing portion of the Supreme Court's jurisdiction. It is true that one of the sources of its jurisdiction is review of cases originating in the district courts under the diversity of citizenship clause and that for a century, during the reign of *Swift v. Tyson*,[6] the federal courts were at liberty to develop a federal common law independent of that of the states. Since the overruling of *Swift v. Tyson* in 1938[7] these common-law cases are transformed into efforts to ascertain the applicable state law; if the lower federal courts have made a diligent effort to do so, the Supreme Court will let the matter rest without review. With the proliferation of federal regulatory and revenue measures and the need for uniformity of interpretation, the task of statutory construction has taken an increasing share of the Court's business. But it is in the area of constitutional law that the Court performs its most distinctive function.

Standing at one remove from the resolution of conflicting pressures and interests through legislation, the Court serves perforce as an arbiter of state and national power and of the claims of government against the individual. In terms of the formalities of the Constitution, the Court is above all concerned with the commerce clause[8] as the instrument of a working federalism and with the Bill of Rights and the Fourteenth Amendment as guarantees of an open society.

It should be said at once that in approaching these profoundly important and delicate tasks the Court is governed less by canons of construction than by philosophic moods. By philosophic mood is not meant personal idiosyncrasy but rather that fusion of a sense of history, of the logical faculty, and of the practical ends in view which must in some subtle balance serve the judge in the judicial process. In its most enduring and memorable work, the Court has been careful not to read the provisions of the Constitution like a last will and testament, lest indeed they become one. Instead, the justices have been guided by the basic canon of Marshall, calculated to turn the mind away from canons: "This provision is made in a constitution, intended to endure for ages to come, and consequently, to be adapted to the various *crises* of human affairs." [9] It was in the tradition of Marshall that Holmes gave expression to his philosophy of constitutional adjudication, when, in speaking of the scope of the treaty-making power, he said:

> . . . when we are dealing with words that also are a constituent act, like the Constitution of the United States, we must realize that they have called into life a being the development of which could not have been foreseen completely by the most gifted of its begetters. It was enough for them to realize or to hope that they had created an organism; it has taken a century and has cost their successors much sweat and blood to prove that they created a nation. The case before us must be considered in the light of our whole experience and not merely in that of what was said a hundred years ago.[10]

The procedural guarantees, in Holmes's view, were to be similarly taken:

> . . . the provisions of the Constitution are not mathematical formulas having their essence in their form; they are organic living institutions transplanted from English soil. Their significance is vital not formal; it is to be gathered not simply by taking the words and a dictionary, but by considering their origin and the line of their growth.[11]

In the same tradition Chief Justice Hughes, dealing with the obligation of contract clause, voiced the organic conception of the Constitution:

It is no answer to say that this public need was not apprehended a century ago, or to insist that what the provision of the Constitution meant to the vision of that day it must mean to the vision of our time. If by the statement that what the Constitution meant at the time of its adoption it means to-day, it is intended to say that the great clauses of the Constitution must be confined to the interpretation which the framers, with the conditions and outlook of their time, would have placed upon them, the statement carries its own refutation.[12]

The commerce clause—the mechanism by which, as has been said, the Court strives to maintain a working federalism—has furnished a vivid illustration of the Court's response to the task of constitutional decision. Three interrelated problems are presented: the scope of the power of Congress, the extent of the power of the states in the silence of Congress, and the effect upon state power of an exercise of Congressional authority.

The first problem was dramatized in the early New Deal period. A majority of the Court, over the protests of Justices Brandeis, Stone, and Cardozo, and on occasion of Chief Justice Hughes, attempted to measure the extent of national authority by such talismanic phrases as "direct" and "indirect" effects on interstate commerce. In so doing it struck down, for example, an act regulating labor relations in the bituminous coal industry, although a conspiracy on the part of miners to stop the flow of shipments had been recognized as falling within the federal antitrust laws.[13] One need not have been a historical determinist to predict that no simple verbal antinomy was powerful enough to stem the tide of national power over activities local in character but having palpable effects on national trade and transportation. Nor need one be a cynic, professing that a switch in time saved nine when the President's Court reorganization plan was introduced, to understand the course of decision from 1937 on, sustaining every measure of national control over the economy.[14]

The problem of state power in the silence of Congress had given rise in the mid-nineteenth century to similar brave but doomed efforts at solution through phrases. For a time it was thought that state laws promoting local health or safety could be sustained because they were not regulations of commerce even though to the pragmatic eye they had all the effects on interstate trade that would have flowed from the same measures if designated commercial. The Court has long since abandoned the merely verbal criteria and has sought, on a highly particularistic basis, to weigh the local benefit and need against the burden on commerce with other states. In the silence of Congress a state may enforce a full-crew law against an interstate railroad; but it may not apply a maximum-train-length statute to such a carrier.[15] The difference can be found only in an estimate, based on a detailed record, of the balance in each case between local safety and the burdensome effects of compliance.[16] Similarly, no monosyllabic answer can be given to the question whether a state may impose a license requirement upon an interstate business; if the grant of the license turns on factors of commercial competition, it will probably be struck down, while if it turns on the financial reliability or sanitary standards of the enterprise in its dealings with local customers, it may well be sustained.[17]

There is, finally, the problem of the effect of affirmative Congressional action on the authority of the states. This effect, in turn, has a double aspect. On the one hand, an act of Congress which "occupies the field" supersedes inconsistent state legislation. But what is meant by the quoted phrase turns once more on a precise analysis of the national policy and the practical effect of the state law on the carrying out of that policy. On the other hand, Congress may elect to use its power not to extend but to contract the scope of national authority. That is, Congress may authorize the states to act upon interstate commerce in ways that would be held to be precluded in the silence of Congress. This technique presents theoretical difficulties that were serious enough to lead President Taft to veto on constitutional grounds the Webb-Kenyon Act, which permitted any state to penalize the importation into it of intoxicating liquors.[18] Various objections could be raised: that Congress may not "delegate" its power over interstate commerce; that Congress may not "regulate" commerce in a nonuniform way; and that since in certain other clauses, notably with respect to state taxation of imports and exports, the Constitution explicitly permits the states to act with the consent of Congress, the maxim *expressio unius* precludes validation by consent under the commerce clause. These objections have been unavailing. The theoretical justification is perhaps best put in terms of the paramount standard of the intention of Congress: In the silence of Congress the Court must hazard the putative intention, while when Congress speaks the judgment of the Court yields to that of Congress in striking a balance between national and state interests. Congress may "regulate" by silence, by extension of its authority, or by permissive sanction to the states.

The result has been an enormously flexible and resourceful federalism. Its value can be seen in the treatment of public control of insurance. For a long time it was generally supposed that the making of insurance contracts was not interstate commerce. In 1944, departing from a body of dicta and assumptions, the Court held that the business of insurance was interstate commerce subject to the Sherman Antitrust Act.[19] This decision placed in some jeopardy the complex pattern of state legislation which had been worked out on the premise that insurance was not interstate commerce. A solution was found, making the best of both worlds of regulation, when Congress promptly enacted a law in the pattern of the earlier legislation on intoxicating liquors, authorizing the states to tax and regulate insurance without regard to its interstate character.[20]

Co-operative federalism has taken many forms, not all of them derived from the commerce clause. Under the power to tax and spend, Congress may make grants to the states upon conditions that are relevant to the federal purposes. Congress may provide a credit for taxpayers against federal taxes on condition that payments are made by the taxpayer under appropriate conditions to his state; this has furnished the co-operative pattern of federal-state unemployment insurance legislation, under which premiums paid to a federally approved state fund are credited against the employer's federal social security tax.[21] Modes of co-operation have been worked out also in the sphere of judicial administration. The federal district courts regularly hear diversity of citizenship cases instituted there or removed from a state court, where the cause of action may rest wholly on state law. Conversely, Congress may require the state courts to entertain causes of action under federal law, at least where the state tribunals have competence to adjudicate comparable cases under their own law.[22] The interlacing patterns may be wanting in clarity and sharpness, but they serve to meet the basic need for modes of organization that avoid both the Balkanization of a loose confederation and the ultimate centralization of a unitary state. Within wide limits the United States may experiment with the processes of federalism. And, as Mr. Justice Johnson observed more than a century ago, "The science of government . . . is the science of experiment." [23]

When we turn from problems of federalism to the relations between the individual and his government, we find that the experimental mood of the Court now tolerates the widest range of legislation, save in one sphere. Within the past two decades, social and economic legislation of state or nation has almost never been struck down under the due process clause of the

Fifth or Fourteenth Amendment; but legislation restricting the freedom of speech or assembly or religion has frequently succumbed to the prohibitions of the First Amendment and of the Fourteenth, which has absorbed and made applicable to the states the provisions of the First.[24]

The difference in treatment has been justified in a number of ways. It has been pointed out that the guarantees of the First Amendment are more explicit than the standards of reasonableness which the courts have drawn from the vague language of the due process clause;[25] that freedom of expression is the matrix, the indispensable condition, for the flourishing of other freedoms;[26] and that restrictions on liberty of expression tend to clog the very political processes that are normally relied on for peaceful change and that offer a democratic alternative to the judicial veto of legislation.[27] The problem of the double standard of judicial review will be explored elsewhere in these essays. It may simply be noted as a fact that there has been a Copernican revolution since the late nineteenth and early twentieth century: whereas formerly the Court (always over the dissents of some of its most respected members) was quick to strike down novel measures of economic and social reform in the name of due process of law and was slow to assimilate the First Amendment freedoms into the Fourteenth, today no real barrier is raised against legislative experiments in the economy but very severe obstacles face legislative restrictions on the launching of ideas.

## III. *The Court as Symbol*

The prestige of the Court has fluctuated widely during its history. It has never escaped the tensions that beset an evolving society. Indeed, it has reflected and articulated those dilemmas and has contributed in the process to the anthology of statesmanship. Its intellectual contribution derives basically from the fact that the Court must generalize and particularize at the same time. Its relative detachment provides an opportunity for dispassionate reflection, which, however, can never be far removed from the concrete instances of conflict that obtrude themselves for decision. In part the special quality of its contribution rests on the tradition of free dissenting opinions. The role of the Court in the intellectual history of the country has nowhere been better recognized than by the philosopher Alexander Meiklejohn, who has written:

> And to us who labor at that task of educating Americans it becomes, year by year, more evident that the Supreme Court has a large part to play in our national teaching. That court is commissioned to interpret to us our own purposes, our own meanings. To a self-governing community it must make clear what, in actual practice, self-governing is. And its teaching has peculiar importance because it interprets principles of fact and of value, not merely in the abstract, but also in their bearing upon the concrete, immediate problems which are, at any given moment, puzzling and dividing us. But it is just those problems with which any vital system of education is concerned. And for this reason, the court holds a unique place in the cultivating of our national intelligence. Other institutions may be more direct in their teaching influence. But no other institution is more deeply decisive in its effect upon our understanding of ourselves and our government.[28]

It is no doubt inescapable that our strongest presidents should have clashed repeatedly with our strongest justices. Marshall managed to bring the Court safely through the storms of Jeffersonian and Jacksonian criticism. Taney, at the end of his judicial career, set himself hopelessly but resolutely against the martial rule countenanced by Lincoln during the Civil War. Theodore Roosevelt campaigned for the recall of judges and of judicial decisions. Franklin D. Roosevelt, his program of reconstruction thwarted by a solid phalanx of five, struck out at the Court and succeeded in educating the profession and the public, whether in agreement or disagreement, on the problems raised by judicial supremacy in a popular government.

It is as true as most truisms to say that the quality of the institution depends not alone on its traditions but on the character of the individuals who man it. Partisan considerations in the appointment of justices have, on the whole, been subordinated. This is not to say, of course, that the general outlook of an appointee has been or should be irrelevant in his selection, but only that narrow political or geographic factors have not been allowed to predominate.[29] A partisan-minded chief executive might reflect sardonically on the unreliability of members of the Court: Story, appointed as a Madisonian Republican, outdid even Marshall in his nationalism; Holmes's lack of enthusiasm for the Sherman Antitrust Act bitterly disappointed the expectations of Theodore Roosevelt; and McReynolds, elevated by Wilson from the attorney generalship, scarcely proved to be a Wilsonian Democrat. When Holmes's place fell vacant, considerations of geography were urged on President Hoover in the interest of the selection of a Westerner. As is reported, Mr. Hoover finally took the advice of Senator Borah of Idaho, who assured him that to the people of that state the most acceptable appointment would be that of Judge Cardozo of New York; in acceding to this wisdom Mr. Hoover performed what was probably the most popular act of his presidency.

That the Court has survived storms and stresses and has over the years strengthened its position has been due, basically, to its tradition of self-scrutiny, re-examination, and self-correction. Mr. Justice Brandeis put concisely the reasons back of this tradition:

> *Stare decisis* is usually the wise policy, because in most matters it is more important that the applicable rule of law be settled than that it be settled right.

> Compare *National Bank* v. *Whitney*, 103 U.S. 99, 102. This is commonly true even where the error is a matter of serious concern, provided correction can be had by legislation. But in cases involving the Federal Constitution, where correction through legislative action is practically impossible, this Court has often overruled its earlier decisions. The Court bows to the lessons of experience and the force of better reasoning, recognizing that the process of trial and error, so fruitful in the physical sciences, is appropriate also in the judicial function.[30]

Chief Justice Taney, witnessing the erosion of doctrine which he thought he had established, was able to convey the sustaining spirit of a living institution:

> After such opinions, judicially delivered, I had supposed that question to be settled, so far as any question upon the construction of the Constitution ought to be regarded as closed by the decision of this court. I do not, however, object to the revision of it, and am quite willing that it be regarded hereafter as the law of this court, that its opinion upon the construction of the Constitution is always open to discussion when it is supposed to have been founded in error, and that its judicial authority should hereafter depend altogether on the force of the reasoning by which it is supported.[31]

## II. CONCORD AND DISCORD

Is the law of the Supreme Court a reflection of the notions of "policy" held by its members? The question recalls the controversy over whether judges "make" or "find" the law. A generation or two ago it was thought rather daring to insist that judges make law. Old Jeremiah Smith, who began the teaching of law at Harvard after a career on the New Hampshire Supreme Court, properly deflated the issue. "Do judges make law?" he repeated. " 'Course they do. Made some myself." Of course Supreme Court justices decide cases on the basis of their ideas of "policy."

But to say this, as to say that judges make law, is not the end but only the beginning of sophistication. For there are levels of policy; and in Supreme Court litigation, values, like troubles, come not single spies but in battalions. In one aspect, a case may present an issue of civil liberties; it may also involve issues of federalism, or of the relation of the Court to the legislature, or of the standing of the litigant to invoke judicial redress at all.

A topical catalog of decisions or of votes of individual justices is likely to focus on the winning and losing litigants and the social interests with which they are identified: big business, taxpayers, labor, political or religious minorities, and so on. To rely on any such scheme of analysis is a dubious approach to an understanding of the Supreme Court. To be sure, there have always been occasions when all other policies or values or interests were submerged in a high tide of feeling on the Court about a particular social cause. One such occasion, which can be viewed with detachment because three quarters of a century have since elapsed, was described by Mr. Justice Miller in his correspondence. It concerned the prolific litigation over state and municipal bonds issued often recklessly in aid of private enterprises after the Civil War. Writing to his brother-in-law, who had been counsel in one of the controversies between bondholders and local taxpayers, Miller described the judicial process in these cases:

> I am sorry to see that you are so much disappointed at the result of your case in our court. It is a result however which I readily foresaw as soon as I discovered that it was a question of a demand growing out of a contract against a municipal corporation.
>
> Our court or a majority of it are, if not monomaniacs, as much bigots and fanatics on that subject as is the most unhesitating Mahometan in regard to his religion. In four cases out of five the case is decided when it is seen by the pleadings that it is a suit to enforce a contract against a city, or town, or a country. If there is a written instrument its validity is a foregone conclusion.[1]

However accurate Miller's description may have been, and however aptly it portrays certain workings of the Court in periods before and since, it will hardly be taken as a picture of the judicial function at its best. To set up similar preferences in contemporary causes as standards of performance for judges is scarcely a service to the administration of justice. Nor is it an adequate basis for an understanding of the work of the Supreme Court.

These essays address themselves, then, not to tabular views on public questions of the day, but to certain questions that are believed to be relevant to an appreciation of the Supreme Court's tasks and decisions. Among the questions are these: How does the framework of democratic federal government within which the Court operates condition its activities? What are the hallmarks of a "liberal" Supreme Court justice? What is the bearing of the strategy and tactics of counsel on the process of constitutional decision? In dramaturgical terms, the chapters may be said to deal with plot, character, and supporting roles. The purpose is not so much to furnish judgments about the Court and its members as to indicate that because of the complexity of the Court's tasks, such judgments are more difficult to reach than might be supposed, and to suggest inquiries relevant in reaching one's own.

To understand the Supreme Court of the United States is a theme that forces lawyers to become philosophers. Alfred North Whitehead, suggesting that the key to a science of values will be found in aesthetics, remarked that the Supreme Court is seeking the aesthetic satisfaction of bringing the Constitution into harmony with the activities of modern America.[2] That is a satisfaction which the Court, in fits of anesthesia, has sometimes denied itself; but no more so than legislatures and executives, upon whom the pleasurable quest equally devolves.

If there is any philosophical problem that finds its special counterpart in the task of the Court, it is the problem of reconciling the One and the Many: one nation and many states; one Supreme Court and many organs of government; one Court speaking with many, often disconcertingly many, voices. In Great Britain, as has been said, the Judicial Committee of the Privy Council always announces its decisions in a single opinion, for the decisions are in the form of advice to the Crown, and the Crown would be confused by conflicting advice. We attribute more hardihood to our bar, fortunately, than the British to their Crown.

The bar has not been entirely receptive to the compliment. Despite the reminder of Chief Justice Hughes that we ought not to expect much greater agreement on the difficult issues that come before the Court than we find in the higher realms of other intellectual disciplines—science, theology, philosophy[3]—we complain that the Many have obscured the One, that Whirl is king, having driven out Zeus. When invited to specify, the bar can draw on statistical tables of division in the Court, catalogued and tabulated with all the deadly precision of a score sheet. It then appears that there are sharp cleavages in the Court in two major areas of decision: the field of civil liberties and the field of application of federal regulatory law. How significant is the discord, and what factors explain it? Unless we look behind the statistical compilations, in which votes are necessarily taken as values, we shall be in danger of emulating those institutes of social studies that my late colleague T. R. Powell once described as places where the counters don't think and the thinkers don't count.

I shall consider first the field of civil liberties, or as it is sometimes described, human rights contrasted with property rights. It is my conviction that the degree of concord in this area is more important then the degree of discord, and that the themes of discord are not, as it were, symmetrical.

The Court as a whole has given sanctuary to civil liberties that were not vindicated even by the Courts on which sat Holmes, Hughes, Brandeis, and Cardozo.

The compulsory flag-salute in public schools, when challenged by a religious objector, was held not to present a substantial constitutional question by a Court that included Hughes and Brandeis. It has now been held, with Justices Roberts, Reed, and Frankfurter dissenting, to violate the Fourteenth Amendment.[4] The all-white primary, when established by rule of a party convention, was held in 1935 by a unanimous Court not to constitute state action in violation of the Fourteenth Amendment. The decision was overruled in 1944, with only Mr. Justice Roberts dissenting.[5] Restrictive covenants forbidding the sale of property to Negroes were until lately enforced in state courts, despite a claim of unconstitutional state action, with the acquiescence of a unanimous Court. Today, with the concurrence of all the Justices who participated in the consideration of the case, such enforcement is held a denial of equal protection of the laws.[6] In passing upon a city's requirement of a permit to speak in a public place, no one on the Court takes refuge in Holmes's early suggestion that because the city owns its parks and common it it has a proprietor's absolute right of exclusion.[7] In upholding the ban on political activities of government employees, contained in the Hatch Act, the Court divided on the outcome, but no member found a complete solution in Holmes's aphorism that there may be a constitutional right to talk politics but not to be a policeman.[8]

Is the Court agreed that civil liberties are to be given a preferred position, that the criteria for deciding the validity of governmental action affecting "human rights" and "property rights" are different? Mr. Justice Frankfurter has protested against the phrase "preferred position," particularly if it implies that under the First Amendment and the due process clause of the Fourteenth there is a presumption of unconstitutionality attaching to any regulation of speech. He has agreed, however, that a judge ought to be readier to find invasion of the Constitution where "free inquiry" is involved than in the "debatable area of economics." "Those liberties of the individual which history has attested as the indispensable conditions of an open as against a closed society," he said, "come to this Court with a momentum for respect lacking when appeal is made to liberties which derive merely from shifting economic arrangements." [9] In short, when freedom of the mind is imperiled by law, it is freedom that commands a momentum of respect; when property is imperiled, it is the lawmakers' judgment that commands respect. This dual standard may not precisely reverse the presumption of constitutionality in civil liberties cases, but obviously it does set up a hierarchy of values within the due process clause.

There is a noteworthy core of agreement on the Court in this realm of values. It is noteworthy because there has been no explicit agreement and little sustained discussion in the Court's opinions touching the basis for this scale of values—whether it is derived from the evidence of history regarding the relative social utility of different kinds of freedom, or is derived from convictions about the nature and duties of man,[10] or from an analysis of representative government.[11] It is the more remarkable because in applying the concept of liberty in the Fourteenth Amendment, the older Courts recognized liberty of contract before acknowledging liberty of speech as entitled to protection.[12] It is remarkable, finally, because other readings of history, other philosophical premises, and above all, other conceptions of the role of the Court can be found in our tradition. Something of this background will be considered in the present chapter; in the following essay a closer view will be taken of the treatment of civil liberties by the Court, and the philosophical grounds that may be advanced for its position.

The most impressive challenge to the double standard has come from Judge Learned Hand, in a memorial address on Chief Justice Stone:

> Even before Justice Stone became Chief Justice [he said] it began to seem as though, when "personal rights" were in issue, something strangely akin to the discredited attitude towards the Bill of Rights of the old apostles of the institution of property was regaining recognition. Just why property itself was not a "personal right" nobody took the time to explain; and perhaps the inquiry would have been regarded as captious and invidious anyway; but the fact remained that in the name of the Bill of Rights the courts were upsetting statutes which were plainly compromises between conflicting interests, each of which had more than a merely plausible support in reason. That looked a good deal as though more specific directions could be found in the lapidary counsels of the Amendments than the successful school had been able to discover, so long as the dispute turned on property. It needed little acquaintance with the robust and loyal character of the Chief Justice to foretell that he would not be content with what to him was an opportunistic reversion at the expense of his conviction as to the powers of a court. He could not understand how the principle which he had all along supported could mean that, when concerned with interests other than property, the courts should have a wider latitude for enforcing their own predilections than when they were concerned with property itself.[13]

Memorial addresses often provide an even truer insight into the speaker than into the subject; and it is probably safer that the views so pointedly put by Judge Hand be ascribed to himself than to the late Chief Justice. At all events, Judge Hand has contributed to clarity of analysis by reminding us that the relevant comparison is not between the enduring values of free inquiry and expression on the one hand, and transitory measures for the control of property on the other; the problem is harder than that. We are obliged to compare the ultimate values of property with those of free inquiry and expression, or to compare the legislative compromises in the two realms; for laws dealing with libel or sedition or sound trucks or a nonpolitical civil service are as truly adjustments and accommodations as are laws fixing prices or making grants of monopolies.

Judge Hand's insistence on equality of values in constitutional decision can be matched by a persistent current of political thought. Indeed, the view that property itself is the matrix, the seedbed that must be conserved if other values are to flourish, has always had expression in American society. One need not revert to the Middle Ages, when, as Maitland observed, English constitutional law was a branch of the law of real property. Nor need one go to the modern philosophical Marxists to be told that personal liberties are but a reflection of the arrangements and pressures and powers in economic life. "Property must be secured," wrote John Adams, "or liberty cannot exist." [14] "The moment the idea is admitted into society," he warned, "that property is not as sacred as the laws of God, and that there is not a force of law and public justice to protect it, anarchy and tyranny commence." [15] And Adams's great antagonist, John Taylor, of Caroline County, Virginia, was just as emphatic: "Is not a power of transferring property by pensions, bounties, corporations and exclusive privileges; and even of bestowing publick money by the unlimited will of legislative bodies, as dangerous to liberty, as a power of doing the same thing by the instrumentality of a privileged church? Is the casuistry consistent, which denies to a government the power of infringing the freedom of religion, and yet invests it with a despotism over the freedom of property? . . . Blackstone has treated of 'the rights of persons, and the rights of things,' but the rights of man include life, liberty and property, according to the prevalent fashion of thinking in the United

States. The last right is the chief hinge upon which social happiness depends. It is therefore extremely important to ascertain, whether it is secured by the same principle with our other rights." Thus John Taylor, the philosopher of agrarian democracy.[16] The debates on suffrage in the 1820's produced some frank and searching inquiries into the role of property. Daniel Webster in Massachusetts and James Kent in New York made statements which have become classic. Said Webster: "Life and personal liberty are, no doubt, to be protected by law; but property is also to be protected by law, and is the fund out of which the means for protecting life and liberty are usually furnished. We have no experience that teaches us, that any other rights are safe, where property is not safe." [17] And Kent, looking about him, was lugubrious, as are the Kents of every age: "My opinion is that the admission of universal suffrage and a licentious press are incompatible with government and security to property, and that the government and character of this country are going to ruin." [18]

Property, indeed, came to have a religious sanction in the evangelism of the gilded age. In 1868, that *annus mirabilis* which gave us at once the Fourteenth Amendment and Cooley's *Constitutional Limitations*, President Hopkins of Williams College published *The Law of Love and Love as Law*. "The Right to Property," he wrote, "reveals itself through an original desire. . . . Without this society could not exist. . . . It will be found too, historically, that the general well-being and progress of society has been in proportion to the freedom of every man to gain property in all legitimate ways, and to security in its possession. . . . The acquisition of property is required by love, because it is a powerful means of benefiting others." [19] Of late the new humanism has insisted on the centrality of property in civilization. Paul Elmer More, in his essay on "Property and Law," advanced this philosophy of history: "Although probably the rude government of barbarous chiefs, when life was precarious and property unimportant, may have dealt principally with wrongs to person, yet the main care of advancing civilization has been for property. After all, life is a very primitive thing. Nearly all that makes it more significant to us than to the beast is associated with our possessions—with property, all the way from the food we share with the beasts, to the most refined products of the human imagination. To the civilized man *the rights of property are more important than the right to life.*" [20]

Of course these encomiums on property have as many meanings as they have motivations. But for all its ambiguities, a concept of property in some form was elevated to first rank by a long line of American figures both influential and unabashed. This strain of thought finds no hospitality on the Court today. To that extent the Justices can share the proud solace of the German artist who exclaimed, "If I am nothing else, at least I am a contemporary!" Certainly it is not discreditable in a judge, even a judge interpreting the Constitution, to be a contemporary. Vistas grow, perspectives lengthen, reflection deepens, and new meanings come to seem fitting for such projecting terms as "liberty" or "due process of law," and "establishment of religion" or "the free exercise thereof." The judge need only be careful not to confuse the heat of the day with a climate of opinion, not to mistake the gusts of a local storm for the steady winds of doctrine. Is not this the answer to be made for judges to the question of the troubled poet who describes a clump of windswept trees and asks:

> Is it as plainly in our living shown
> By bend and twist, which way the wind hath blown?

Of late, it must be confessed, the new liberty has grown to such a flourishing estate that at times it seems to embrace a new property in the guise of freedom of speech and assembly. The transformation of economic pressures into rights of free expression has been partially accomplished in labor controversies. Picketing is indeed a hybrid, comprising elements of persuasion, information, and publicity, together with elements of nonverbal conduct, economic pressure, and signals for predetermined action. Because of its localization, moreover, it is unlike ordinary public speech in requiring certain hearers to disclose their response. It is scarcely surprising that judgments on the Court should differ on the weight to be accorded these elements in fixing the point at which picketing becomes subject to the state's intervention and control.

There are, however, limits beyond which the new property in the position of organized labor will not be carried. The test came early in 1949. Does labor have a right of association so fundamental that the Constitution draws a line of fire around the power of the union to exclude nonmembers from employment? Are agreements for a closed shop constitutionally immune from the authority of government to regulate or prohibit them? Some observers were inclined to believe that on this issue the Court would be sorely rent. And yet with the concurrence of all the Justices who participated in the case the Court sustained the authority of the state to prohibit closed-shop agreements, at least where the state also prohibits interference by employers with the organization of labor.[21] The position of the union toward the parasitic nonjoiner is no more sacrosanct than the position of the employer toward the union members.

The Court is doubtless as aware as the rest of us that the effective enjoyment of civil liberties requires a degree of command over material resources, just as the exercise of virtue assumes the practical capacity to choose one satisfaction and reject another. As Professor Hocking has judiciously put it: "To contemporary consciousness it has become an axiom that there can be *no freedom without provision;* for a large part of mankind the main task of freedom is at the economic level; and business, as Beardsley Ruml has shown, has to share this task with politics. But it remains true that provision, work, and leisure are not enough; the most abundant provision is not human freedom unless a man remains the unhampered director of his powers of thought and action. Concrete freedom requires both factors." [22] The difficulty of translating this into constitutional terms is the dangerous impropriety of committing to the Court the task of defining minimum standards of material provision.

And so the Court has left to the forum of political action the major issue of our time, how far economic community is essential to human freedom. The Constitution enforces no answer, equal protection of the laws in its narrow sense apart, though the question is an old one for the makers of constitutions. On May 1, 1949, we celebrated (or we should have) the three hundredth anniversary of that remarkable product of the Puritan Revolution and its army, *An Agreement of the Free People of England.* This seminal document, the final version of the platform of the Leveller group, foreshadowed universal manhood suffrage, religious toleration, the abolition of imprisonment for debt, and other of our modern guarantees; but it also provided that "it shall not be in the power of any Representative, in any wise, to . . . level men's estates, destroy Propriety, or make all things Common." [23] If we take pride in the modernity of the authors of this document, Lilburne, Walwyn, Prince, and Overton, we may also take counsel at the modernity of their treatment: for they were denounced with the hateful epithet of the day, "Levellers"; and the document itself was drafted in the cells of the Tower of London.

The Levellers were answered by the left wing of the Puritan reformers, whose symbol was their digging in St. George's Hill to convert it into a collective farm.

In 1652 appeared the Diggers' *Law of Freedom in a Platform*, which analyzed the essentials of liberty: "Some say, It [Freedom] lies in the free use of Trading, and to have Patents, Licenses, and Restraints removed: But this is a Freedom under the Will of a Conqueror. Others say, It is true Freedom to have Ministers to preach, and for people to hear whom they will, without being restrained or compelled from or to any form of worship: But this is an unsettled Freedom. . . . True Commonwealths Freedom lies in the Free Enjoyment of the Earth." [24]

Our Constitution and our judges have left our St. George's Hills to be acquired or not as the legislature may decide; if one is acquired as a common, it may have to be opened to the speeches of Diggers of all persuasions, though not to their implements of labor. This is the dominant harmony within the Court today.

There are, of course, themes of discord in the score of the modern Court. But just as it would be idle to close our ears to these themes, so it would be a distortion to hear them as a single discord. There are at least three distinct lines of conflict, it seems to me, in the area of civil liberties.

The first lies in the relative regard given to what may be called aggressive and passive liberties. On the whole, the active proselyting interests have been given greater sanctuary than the quiet virtues or the right of privacy. The emergence of the militant sect of Jehovah's Witnesses dramatized this conflict. A fairly stable majority of one shielded the Witnesses from nondiscriminatory taxes on their distribution of literature, from local ordinances forbidding the ringing of doorbells by solicitors, and from regulations requiring permits for the use of sound trucks.[25] The Court here has acted virtually as a legislative drafting bureau for municipal authorities. The zeal of Jehovah's Witnesses can be kept within bounds by properly framed regulations. Notice posted by the householder himself that he does not wish to be disturbed may be made the basis for criminal prosecution if the notice is disregarded. And sound trucks can be regulated in the matter of decibels and the hours of their use. While in the control of economic activities a government may extend its regulatory hand beyond the strict necessities of the problem, at least as those necessities might appear to a judge, the control of evangelism must be virtually the least possible control needed to achieve the result. The states are somewhat in the legal position of the individual who may act in self-defense if he uses no more force than necessary.

While the privilege of righteous peaceful aggression has thus been sanctified, the privilege of private belief and of security from intrusion has been qualified. A religious objector to war is unable by reason of his belief to become a member of the bar of Illinois, and the Supreme Court approves because he cannot conscientiously subscribe to the state constitution, which authorizes the calling out of militia, even though it has been traditional in practice to exempt genuinely conscientious objectors and even though the state has reserved the power to punish disobedience in an actual emergency.[26] Moreover, the immunity from unreasonable search and seizure has had only wavering protection. It is worth more than passing note that the majority in the cases of aggressive liberties has sometimes dissolved when freedom from search and seizure is challenged, so that it has on occasion fallen to the lot of a differently constituted group to vindicate this liberty, which can fairly be deemed basic to many others.[27] For in a police state there can be few if any liberties more obnoxious and indeed impossible than the liberty to record and transmit one's thoughts in private without fear of the unchecked official eavesdropper.

In sum, there are civil liberties that point to insurgency and there are those that look to integrity of the person. Whether by reason of temperament or experience or the variant readings of history, different judges have found in these realms different constitutional accommodations between liberty and authority.

The second theme of discord turns on the clear-and-present-danger test, the criterion that would prevent any official interference with speech unless the speech presents a clear and present danger of some harm that the state may control. One group on the Court finds in this criterion a standard for judging most limitations on human expression; others believe that the test is frequently inapt. The conflict is exemplified when the test is used to mark the province of speech uttered about a judge or about a case before him. Does the Constitution render the publication of threatening language immune from punishment as contempt of court unless there is a clear and present danger that the judgment of the judge will be distorted and the even-handed administration of justice corrupted? Or is the temperate and undisturbed administration of justice itself so fundamental a value in the safeguarding of civil liberties that speech may be punished which is calculated to deflect the judicial judgment even though there is no showing that in the particular instance deflection was a clear and present danger?

The clear-and-present-danger test had its origin with Mr. Justice Holmes in sedition cases. It is apparent that he found in the test a useful measure of the range of free discussion where our institutions are challenged in the public forum. The test is pretty clearly drawn from the criminal law, and in particular, from the analysis of it by Holmes as scholar and state court judge;[28] for the criminal law is necessarily concerned with the line at which innocent preparation ends and a guilty conspiracy or attempt begins. These standards of proximity and degree, as Holmes called them, were made to do service in constitutional law in marking the line between innocent talk and guilty incitement to action. The state may not punish open talk, however hateful; not for the hypocritical reason that Hyde Parks are a safety valve, but because a bit of sense may be salvaged from the odious by minds striving to be rational, and this precious bit will enter into the amalgam that we fashion. At least that is our faith, and if we are reminded that the irrational element furnishes the more powerful charge in the process of transmutation, we may answer that we dare not concentrate the whole enterprise in a few censors whose pathology may be even more fatal.

But the test is founded on the importance of persuasion by unfettered and contentious talk in an open forum. It would not be applied today to protect a voluble atheist during services in a church. It was not applied in Holmes's day to statements made out of court in an effort to sway a magistrate whose office is meant to insulate him from precisely such pressures. It is hardly surprising that those judges on the Court who value relatively highly what I have called the quiet virtues are the judges who have insisted that the integrity of the judicial function may be safeguarded by law without a showing of clear and present danger.[29]

The lines of division were broken down again in passing on the validity of the Hatch Act. In that Act Congress had weighed more highly the value of a disinterested public service than the value of full political activity by government employees. The relevant provisions of the Act were sustained, and some of the judges who insisted upon the clear-and-present-danger test as applied to contempt of court were nevertheless willing to appraise these restrictions on political activity of civil servants without inquiring whether such activity put public administration definitely and imminently in jeopardy.[30]

The clear-and-present-danger test is a useful criterion of illicit speech where the social harm apprehended from the speech would flow from the effect of the ideas conveyed. In such cases, if there is time for counter-persuasion, the test is a safeguard against premature intervention by the state on the basis of speculation in historical futures. Even the reminder of the psychologists that verbal impacts may not be wholly eradicable need not, on balance, preclude this guarantee of the free play of ideas. But the test is not appropriate where the harm is such that a corrective could not be sought through countervailing speech: contempt of court, pornography, and political activities by civil servants are examples. Perhaps the fetish that has been made of the test in some quarters has been responsible for an overreaction against it in areas where it could appropriately be employed.

Even where it is appropriate, the clear-and-present-danger test is an oversimplified judgment unless it takes account also of a number of other factors: the relative seriousness of the danger in comparison with the value of the occasion for speech or political activity; the availability of more moderate controls than those the state has imposed; and perhaps the specific intent with which the speech or activity is launched. No matter how rapidly we utter the phrase "clear and present danger," or how closely we hyphenate the words, they are not a substitute for the weighing of values. They tend to convey a delusion of certitude when what is most certain is the complexity of the strands in the web of freedoms which the judge must disentangle.

A third issue dividing the Court is the relevance of federalism in the vindication of civil liberties. In enforcing civilized standards of criminal procedure the Court as a whole has found greater warrant for intervention in cases of federal than of state convictions. The now celebrated *McNabb* rule,[31] excluding from evidence confessions obtained while the prisoner is held by federal authorities without prompt arraignment, has no counterpart in cases from the state courts, where some element of actual coercion must be shown in order to exclude a confession.[32] The *McNabb* case is a judge-made rule of evidence enforcing a federal legislative rule of arraignment. Mr. Justice Frankfurter wrote the opinion with only Mr. Justice Reed dissenting. In these cases of criminal procedure it is not uncommon to find this alignment, but with a shifting majority; while in picketing cases the two justices' roles in finding immunity are reversed. It was Mr. Justice Reed who wrote the Court's opinion and Mr. Justice Frankfurter who dissented in the tragic case of *Fisher v. United States*,[33] sustaining the death sentence imposed on a semiliterate Negro for a killing that the jury might well have found was unpremeditated had the trial judge guided the jury with the psychological perception shown in the dissenting opinion in the Supreme Court. Mr. Justice Frankfurter has given voice to his impatience with the Court's readiness to review state decisions at the behest of those who excite our sympathies, where the state procedures were not properly observed in pressing the claim of unfairness. The Court is not, he has said bluntly, a super-legal-aid bureau.[34] And yet in cases like Fisher's, arising in a lower federal court, he has been ready to employ the supervisory power of the Court to enforce meticulously fair standards in criminal trials. Likewise, on the side of substantive federal criminal law, he has shown sensitivity to the abuses that inhere in the facile use of conspiracy charges as a means of cumulating sentences and of making all too complex the procedural task of individual defendants.[35]

The problem of the standards governing the states has been enmeshed in the controversy over the issue whether the Fourteenth Amendment embodies the entire national Bill of Rights. Mr. Justice Black has fought valiantly to establish this proposition notwithstanding over half a century of adjudication to the contrary. Indeed this effort, buttressed with great historical research in the *Adamson* case,[36] appears to be the culmination of a persistent search by Mr. Justice Black for a textual basis on which to predicate the maximum protection of civil liberties with a modicum of protection for interests of property. Other members of the Court have employed a double standard for interests of personality and property on philosophic grounds, but Mr. Justice Black is understandably apprehensive that such a measure of values may be fleeting over a period of time. He would therefore reject standards for which he reserves that most opprobrious epithet "natural law," [37] in favor of the compulsion of the constitutional words themselves, if in the light of language and history they can bear his reading.

Early in his justiceship he advanced the view that the "persons" protected by the due process clause of the Fourteenth Amendment are natural persons and not corporations.[38] But how were the civil liberties of natural persons to be safeguarded under the protection of "life, liberty, and property" in the due process clause unless the economic interests of such persons were to claim parallel treatment? A tentative answer seems to have been ventured in *Hague v. C.I.O.* Although the rights of assembly and freedom of speech were upheld by a majority of the Court, in a separate opinion Justices Roberts and Black united in placing the result on the "privileges and immunities of citizens of the United States" rather than the due process clause.[39] Mr. Justice Black was apparently reconciled to the conclusion that such protection under the privileges and immunities clause would be limited to citizens of the United States, excluding aliens as well as corporations; but at the same time, the clause might be interpreted to include the civil liberties enumerated in the first eight Amendments without extending the same cloak of protection to economic interests under the due process clause; that clause would presumably be left as a guarantee simply of procedural justice.

This revival of the privileges and immunities clause

was put to the test in reviewing the contempt convictions of Harry Bridges and the *Los Angeles Times*. A case could hardly have been more fiendishly conceived for the purpose of testing the source of the guarantee of freedom of speech and press, since the petitioners were respectively an alien and a corporation. The Court in an opinion by Mr. Justice Black found it possible to reverse the conviction on Fourteenth Amendment grounds; but without specifically replying to the pointed inquiry of the dissenters who asked to be informed just what clause of the Fourteenth Amendment was being invoked.[40] Finally, in the *Adamson* case, the inquiry was met by the assertion in the dissent of Mr. Justice Black that the provisions of the first section of the Fourteenth Amendment, taken "separately, and as a whole," incorporate the national Bill of Rights.[41] This position, which has not commended itself to a majority of the Court, would achieve to the utmost the objectives suggested a little earlier: a guarantee of civil liberties to all individuals, citizens and aliens; a residue of procedural guarantees in the vague and inclusive due process clause; and the relegation of substantive economic interests to the discard of "natural law."

But it is one thing to slam the door of the due process clause, and another to keep it shut. Of the four Justices who joined in the *Adamson* dissent, two—Justices Murphy and Rutledge—were explicit in serving notice that the Bill of Rights provides content, but only a minimum content, for the Fourteenth Amendment. Abuses may be unconstitutional though not specifically enumerated and described. And even Justices Black and Douglas, the other two members of the group, are not satisfied, as Professor John Frank has acutely observed, to rest on the specific guarantees of the first eight Amendments; for they are no less persuaded than their brethren that, for example, criminal statutes may be unconstitutional when they are too vague and indefinite to form a guide to conduct, although there is nothing in the text of the Bill of Rights which denounces laws on that score, save as the standard may be smuggled into the due process clause.[42]

Likewise the self-incrimination clause of the Fifth Amendment offers only a delusively greater certainty than the due process standard. The former guarantee is clearly violated by compelling the defendant to give testimony in court. But how does the clause dispense with judgments of fairness and unfairness when the question is the admissibility of evidence extracted from the defendant by a stomach pump, or of blood samples or strands of hair taken without his consent, or when the defendant is asked to rise in the courtroom, or to put on a cap, for purposes of identification? Some of these issues have divided the Court; but it is hard to see how they could be resolved more objectively through resort to the more specific terms of self-incrimination rather than to the more general criterion of due process of law. The element of judgment is inescapable once the privilege of self-incrimination is applied beyond the case of verbal testimony.

One man's natural law may turn out to be his critic's fighting verities. A righteous repudiation of natural law is apt to recall T. H. Huxley's renunciation of rhetoric: "Let me observe, in passing, that rhetorical ornament is not in my way, and that gilding refined gold would, to my mind, be less objectionable than varnishing the fair face of truth with that pestilent cosmetic, rhetoric." [43]

The whole episode of the debate on the general meaning of the Fourteenth Amendment is unfortunate. The controversy magnifies differences and obscures agreements. The Court is agreed that the Amendment protects aliens and corporations (at least when they conduct a newspaper business). The Court is hardly concerned with the question whether a specific guarantee in the Bill of Rights, like the Seventh Amendment's guarantee of a jury in civil cases involving more than twenty dollars, shall be made applicable to the states by the Fourteenth.

As a controversy over the meaning of history, the debate on the Fourteenth Amendment can hardly be resolved. Whatever the general language of the sponsors of the Amendment, they did not squarely address themselves to the question whether each and every enumerated right in the first eight Amendments was meant to be carried into the Fourteenth; and much less can we find an answer in the views of the legislators who ratified in the states. Besides, the states have adapted their procedures on the assumption that there was room for experimentation, particularly in the substitution of other forms for the grand jury. And the guarantee against self-incrimination hardly demands slavish adoption by the states of all the peripheral rules that have grown up around the practice in the federal courts, so long as confessions obtained by coercing the will are ruled out, as they are, under the due process clause.

The pressing issues center on unlawful searches and seizures and on the right of indigent defendants in criminal cases to have counsel appointed as a matter of course.

The issuc of evidence that is obtained by a search or seizure conducted by state officials which would be unconstitutional if done by federal officers might have been resolved in a number of ways. For many years it was held that such evidence was admissible in state courts, whether because the guarantee against unreasonable searches and seizures in the Fourth Amendment had no application to state officers or because, even if it had, the states were free to follow the common-law rule of admissibility of illegally obtained evidence. A pincers movement has now enveloped this position. On one side there were decisions holding that evidence obtained by particularly shocking methods (the stomach pump involuntarily used, for example) was inadmissible in a state court. And in 1960 the Court decided that evidence obtained through an unreasonable state search violated the Fourteenth Amendment and hence was inadmissible in a federal court. The two lines of attack converged in 1961, when the Court held that the fruits of an unreasonable state search are inadmissible in evidence in a state court.[44] Even this outcome was not clarified or entailed by the theory of incorporation of the entire Bill of Rights into the Fourteenth Amendment. Mr. Justice Black, one of the group of five constituting the majority, was able to concur only by relying on the Fifth Amendment privilege against self-incrimination as well as on the Fourth, although the privilege itself has not been held by the Court to be incorporated in the Fourteenth.

The issue of the right to counsel has had an evolution that may not be wholly closed. In the federal courts the right to have counsel appointed for indigent defendants has been required since 1938, on the ground that it is commanded by the Sixth Amendment.[45] A majority of the Court has been unwilling to apply this blanket rule to state prosecutions, preferring a case-by-case review looking to the essential fairness or unfairness of the procedure.[46] One may hope that a majority of the Court will turn to the view that the appointment of counsel is as indispensable to the just and even-handed administration of the criminal law in the state courts as in the federal courts. It would be helped to reach this conclusion by avowing frankly that the Sixth Amendment does not furnish the real reason for the requirement in the federal courts. It seems more nearly true to regard that Amendment as having simply conferred the right on the accused to employ counsel—a right that of course was by no means assured prior to the adoption of the Constitution. If the right to have counsel appointed in the federal courts is acknowledged to rest on a pervasive sense of justice, it should be extended to state prosecutions as an element of due process of law. This would be a happy denouement of the dramatic, the overdramatic, clash over the Fourteenth Amendment which has drawn so heavily on the energies of the Court.

These cleavages in the Court—on aggressive and passive liberties, on the clear-and-present-danger test, and on the relevance of federalism—significant as they are, hardly constitute a Great Divide. Intensity of feeling, however, generally varies inversely with the distance separating the disputants, and more obloquy has usually been heaped on heretics than on infidels.

It is not remarkable that the process of constitutional decision has become more self-conscious, more avowedly an expression of political philosophy, than ever before. Our present judges have gone to school, as it were, to Holmes and Cardozo. And they are as aware as the rest of us that clichés are paper-weight weapons in a world of colliding civilizations. What is perhaps more remarkable is that the process of statutory construction has likewise become an aspect of political philosophy.

The familiar canons and maxims of interpretation, if not paper thin, are at all events wooden. Not even Maitland's compression of the canons to five jocular words in describing his practice as a member of the Council of the Senate of Cambridge University is a wholly reliable guide: "I always stretch a statute" [47]—though some would no doubt insist that it explains as well as anything else the current practice of the Court.

The treatment of statutes is a philosophical exercise because it is another aspect of the Many and the One—one state, many organs, of which the judiciary is one. A recurring pattern of conflict will describe the judge's problem: How far is a court free to reconsider an earlier doubtful decision when the legislature meanwhile has not acted to change the law? The question is thrust on the Court in many manifestations. Does the Sherman

Act now encompass insurance contracts, though the making of them was assumed in 1890 not to be interstate commerce and the Act has not been amended?[48] Does an income tax expressly laid on dividends to the extent permitted by the Sixteenth Amendment authorize a tax on all stock dividends when at the time of the statute only a limited class had been held constitutionally taxable?[49] Does the Naturalization Act, repeating earlier language requiring the applicant to support and defend the Constitution and laws of the United States against all enemies, foreign and domestic, authorize an oath to bear arms to be exacted of a conscientious objector, when the earlier law had been so construed by a divided Court?[50] Does the Mann Act apply to polygamy, when the Court had held it to include noncommercial vice?[51] Each of the earlier decisions had been roundly criticized. Should a judge's impulse toward self-correction be checked because of apparent acquiescence by Congress in the original sin? The answer should depend on a closer examination of the legislature's inaction in the particular case, and on the viability of an overruling decision. It is not so important how these questions are answered as it is that they be asked.

I have heard it said that the courts should always leave the function of correction to the legislature; that as this is in the legislature's power, it is the legislature's business. But surely this is a gross overstatement. The legislature's inaction may reflect satisfaction with the fluidity of the judicial process rather than with the particular precedent. The legislature may be reluctant to pose a constitutional issue too sharply, as where it prefers not to make general statutory language explicitly retroactive, or where it retains broad constitutional terms in a statute without specific amendment. To defer to the legislature in these circumstances would be playing an Alphonse-Gaston game.

I have also heard it suggested, at the other extreme,

that the courts should wholly disregard legislative inaction, for self-correction is the proper business of judges, and we are meant to be ruled by the directions of the old legislature as judges from time to time fathom those directions, until the living legislature acts positively with all the proper formalities. But at the very least the inaction of Congress in the face of strong pressure to change the law may well lead judges to consider whether their decisions were as egregiously wrong as they might otherwise suppose. Moreover, action and inaction are only convenient terms of degree. A specific vote rejecting an amendment to the law is, to be sure, positive and formal action, though even this may be explained away on the evidence as a choice to leave the matter open-ended for the courts. Short of such a specific vote, there may be a reconsideration of the larger legislative problem, eventuating in a new act without any formal statutory reference to the point of the Court's decision. This nevertheless provides a new starting point, a pointer held in living hands, and the silence of the statute on the precise issue becomes relevant and must be interpreted by some such analysis of internal evidence as I have suggested.

Some members of the Court are more sensitive to legislative silences than others. They are more sensitive, too, to what I have called the problem of the viability of an overruling decision. Will it leave in its wake so great a wreckage that the business is best left to the legislature, which can act prospectively or can make the needed adjustments to remove inequities? Mr. Justice Douglas in the stock dividend case said that such considerations are "none of our business." [52] But when judgment is poised, the consequences can scarcely be disregarded as part of judicial statecraft. It is significant that on a number of recent occasions counsel for the government, recognizing the dislocations that would result from the advanced position it was urging on the Court, took pains to assert that it had obtained informal assurances from administrative or legislative leaders that remedial regulations or legislation would be sponsored to take care of inequities. It is even more significant that on each occasion this argument was thrown back at its proponents by a segment of the Court, particularly Justices Jackson and Frankfurter, who retorted that the whole matter should be left to Congress if the shattering of precedent by the Court would leave debris that Congress would have to clear away.[53]

The consequences to be expected from an overruling decision are relevant, but the inability or unwillingness of Congress or the executive to deal with them may at times have been exaggerated. In 1938 the Court abandoned the doctrine of immunity of salaries of state employees from federal taxation.[54] The government had not argued for so sweeping a decision; the taxing statute and the regulations were couched in the most general terms; it was not until the case was pending that the regulations were changed, and then only to include public salaries unless constitutionally immune from taxation; finally, a month before the decision the President felt it advisable to ask Congress for specific legislation, taxing state salaries and waiving immunity of federal salaries from state taxation, declaring, "The Federal Government does not now levy income taxes on the hundreds of thousands of State, county, and municipal employees." [55] Despite this concatenation of cautions the Court made new law. The taxpayer, asking a rehearing, urged that the decision be applied prospectively only, to avoid injustices. Solicitor General Jackson agreed that the Court had power thus to limit its decision but maintained that the problem of caring for inequities should be left to the resourcefulness of administrative regulations and action by Congress.[56] In fact, Congress responded to the problem by enacting the Public Salaries Act of 1939, making the federal tax prospective only, and waiving federal immunity on a similar basis.[57] I suggest that there was wisdom as well as advocacy in the Solicitor General's position.

The implication to be drawn from divisions on these issues is not that those who are laggard in reinterpreting statutes are less hospitable than their brethren to the claims of collectors of internal revenue, or more hostile to the claims of conscientious objectors, or more opposed to controls over restraints of trade. The implication is rather that some members of the Court rebel more sharply at what they conceive to be an effort to push them farther along the road to Utopia than the elected lawmakers have been propelled. In erecting what Judge Learned Hand has aptly called a bias against bias,[58] they may have allowed themselves to be repelled too strongly from their private bent and the advances of their brethren. If anything more is needed to assure a disinterested judgment than a bias against bias, it is perhaps a bias against bias-against-bias. For balance may be lost by leaning backwards as well as forwards, just as deep inner tension may be aggravated by too deliberately trying to combat it.

How can the professional, or indeed the lay, observer of the Court's work better understand the concord and discord that he finds? He can recognize that because of the Court's special position in relation to our political as well as social institutions, it perforce operates in more than one realm of values; and that to assess those values requires judicial art, not artfulness. He can strive to understand the pressures of advocacy and of personal preference and the defensive mechanism that these evoke in the judicial mind. He can endeavor to appreciate the complexities of judging before criticizing the simplicities of voting. He can refrain from assigning judges to appointed places in a heavenly choir, to tiers in a celestial hierarchy. By doing these things we can perhaps give point to the story of the Irish cleric who was asked by a parishioner what the difference was between the cherubim and seraphim, and who answered, "I think that there was once a difference between them, but they have made it up."

★★★

## III. STANDARDS FOR CIVIL LIBERTIES

In the preceding chapter some attention was given to the areas of agreement and disagreement in the Court on issues of civil liberties; in particular, textual and historical considerations were summoned to a discussion of the "double standard" of review of measures affecting economic interests as compared with civil liberties. The subject calls now for fuller treatment, from the standpoint of actual practice and of philosophic justification.

Mr. Justice Jackson offered a wry reminder in 1951 that the experience of the Supreme Court in applying against local authorities the guarantees of free speech—and he might have added the other guarantees of the First Amendment—has been quite brief:

> This Court's prior decisions, as well as its decisions today, will be searched in vain for clear standards by which it does, or lower courts should, distinguish

legitimate speaking from that acknowledged to be outside of constitutional protection. One reason for this absence is that this Court has had little experience in deciding controversies over city control of street meetings. As late as 1922, this Court declared, ". . . neither the Fourteenth Amendment nor any other provision of the Constitution of the United States imposes upon the States any restrictions about 'freedom of speech.' "[1]

The evolution of the enforcement of First Amendment guarantees under the aegis of the Fourteenth is an interesting study in the throwing up of bridges before, and the burning of them behind, characteristic of juridical advance. The protection of property and of liberty of contract had long since been assured under decisions applying the Fourteenth Amendment. The interests of a teacher and of a private school, challenging interference with their pursuits, were well calculated to furnish the span between proprietary and forensic rights.[2] When the span was crossed the newly taken ground provided a new base for advance. Freedom of speech, recognized in 1925 as a guaranteed interest in the *Gitlow* case,[3] was not less to be preserved when it took the form of religious proselyting;[4] and so, in turn, the protection of forensic religious activity led to the inclusion of religious nonobservance in the *Flag Salute* cases; first, as in *Gitlow*, a recognition of the general right but its rejection in the special case, and then an acceptance by decision itself.[5]

Looking back, it is hard to see how the Court could have done otherwise, how it could have persisted in accepting freedom of contract as a guaranteed liberty without giving equal status to freedom of press and speech,[6] assembly,[7] and religious observance.[8] What does not seem so inevitable is the inclusion within the Fourteenth Amendment of the concept of nonestablishment of religion in the sense of forbidding nondiscriminatory aid to religion, where there is no interference with freedom of religious exercise. Whether the First Amendment guarantee against establishment of religion was a peculiarly antinational guarantee, whether nonetheless by 1868 the principle against public aid had so developed as to become part of a state taxpayer's property interest within the Fourteenth Amendment, or whether the true test is rather the crystallized sentiment of the mid-twentieth century, these are debatable and debated questions.[9] For purposes of this essay it is necessary only that these questions be asked, not that they be answered.

Whatever the Court may have lacked in temporal seasoning, to revert to Mr. Justice Jackson's reminder, it has supplied in the intensity of its efforts in recent years. It requires no pedantic use of a calculating machine to discover that in the past twenty-five years the Fourteenth Amendment has had very little impact on the regulation of economic affairs and very great impact on issues of procedure and civil liberties. In undertaking to consider the subject of civil liberties one must acknowledge at the outset that the term covers a variety of interests. The "liberties of the subject," in the English phrase, are of many kinds. As has been suggested earlier, there are energetic liberties—freedom to speak, to petition, to assemble, and to proselyte; and there are more passive liberties—freedom from unwarranted official intrusion, from unreasonable searches and seizures, and from official brutality.

Not only do civil liberties differ in their quality. In some cases it is far from clear with which side the interests of civil liberty are to be identified. When an individual is charged with contempt of court because of publicly uttered admonitions to the judge regarding the outcome of a pending case, is the important civil liberty to be found in the privilege of free expression or in the privilege of litigants to enjoy a hearing before triers whose minds are not tampered with by extrajudicial pressures?[10] When an individual is prosecuted for voting frauds under a statute that must be generously construed to cover the offense, is the interest of civil liberty to be found in the integrity of the suffrage or in the protection of an accused against vague definitions of crime?[11] Fidelity to the principle of civil liberties does not supply a ready answer in such cases. Moreover, even in cases where an issue of civil liberties is clearly identifiable, it must be remembered that the issue is likely to be entwined with others in the litigation. There may be questions of standing to complain, or of procedural lapses in the presentation in the lower courts.[12] There may be doubts regarding the appropriateness of the subject for judicial review, doubts as to feasible judicial standards or judicial sanctions in what are called "political" controversies.[13] A court may not be serving the cause of liberty under law by overstepping its own bounds in order to keep other departments of government within theirs.

When allowance has been made, however, for these complexities, some general views can be ventured concerning the issues of civil liberties in the Supreme Court. In this essay I shall not undertake a catalogue of decisions but shall address myself to three inquiries suggested by the development that has occurred. First, does the Court apply a double standard in the review of civil liberties questions and the review of other questions? Second, is a double standard justified? Third, how effective can Supreme Court review be?

## I. *A Double Standard in Practice*

In *McCulloch v. Maryland* Chief Justice Marshall, discussing the weight to be given to a practice of government long acquiesced in, observed that in the case before him "the great principles of liberty are not concerned." [14] A little more than a hundred years later a judge of the Court of Appeals of the District of Columbia was able to say, "It should be remembered that of the three fundamental principles which underlie government, and for which government exists, the protection of life, liberty, and property, the chief of these is property." [15] Today the phrase of Chief Justice Marshall has a more contemporary ring than that of Mr. Justice Van Orsdel.

To what extent is it true to say that a double standard has of late been applied? It may be useful to examine, with this question in mind, the operation of certain principles of judicial review in constitutional cases.

Perhaps the most basic postulate of judicial review is that the legislature possesses a generous choice of means. In order to prevent littering of the streets the local authorities may elect to forbid the distribution there of all commercial handbills;[16] but though the end would be better served by the prohibition of noncommercial handbills as well, this further step cannot be taken.[17] A legislature may outlaw some edibles and potables that are innocuous in themselves as a matter of administrative convenience in suppressing what is objectionable;[18] yet such marginal enforcement in the realm of publications will not be permitted.[19] On the principle that, in Mr. Justice Brandeis's words, sunlight is the most powerful of all disinfectants, a legislature may require registration, with its attendant publicity, as a means of protecting consumers or investors;[20] yet registration of solicitors for labor unions may not be required as a condition of making a general appeal on behalf of trade unionism.[21]

Nothing is better settled than that the courts will not inquire into the motives of the legislature, and that a rate of taxation graduated according to size or volume is legitimate;[22] yet the circumstances of a Louisiana graduated tax on newspapers make it suspect and impel the Court to strike it down.[23] The courts do not sit to retry facts found by administrative tribunals where rights of property are involved;[24] it is not difficult to discover less deference to the administrative findings in cases touching human freedom.[25] The canons of statutory construction are sufficiently accordionlike to permit an expansive or a contracting view of legislative coverage in the light of the interests affected; one view for dangerous drugs,[26] another for questionable literature.[27] The same fluidity permits the inference of legislative ratification of administrative action to be drawn or to be rejected in the name of a presumption of greater solicitude on the part of the legislature for basic human freedoms.[28] Administrative remedies must be exhausted before a deprivation of rights can be claimed, lest the complainant cry before he is hurt, and there is no presumption that the administrator will abuse his discretion;[29] but where large discretion is reposed in an official to grant or withhold a license to speak or assemble, it is unnecessary to try the temper of the administrator before raising a protest in court.[30] Strict criminal liability, regardless of the defendant's lack of knowledge, may be imposed for violations of the food and drug laws; but that kind of sanction may not be applied to a bookseller having no knowledge of the contents of an obscene book.[31]

Two items call for more elaborate scrutiny: the doctrines, not infrequently advanced, that in matters of civil liberty a prior restraint is more vulnerable than penalties after the act, and that a law abridging civil liberties is to be judged on its face. Each of these presents complexities beneath the surface.

In ordinary regulation a legislature may, and commonly does, include a variety of sanctions—civil penalties, criminal penalties, and injunctions against violation. The antitrust laws and statutory price control are familiar examples. In regulating the liberties of the First Amendment, is the sanction of prior restraint inadmissible? A generation ago an able historian searching the classic legal authorities was able to assert flatly that prior restraints are illegitimate and subsequent punishment is freely available.[32] Chief Justice Hughes in the *Near* case[33] gave the *coup de grâce* to the latter part of this proposition while maintaining that there are special objections to prior restraint. It is now clear that if subsequent penalties may constitute abridgments under the First Amendment, it is also true that some forms of prior restraint may be perfectly proper.[34] Both terms of the Blackstonian formula have been qualified.

Certain distinctions commonly drawn between prior restraint and subsequent punishment will not bear analysis. It is sometimes said that prior restraint is the greater deterrent. This generality depends on the psychological aspects of the case. An injunction running against a particular individual may, to be sure, deter him more sharply than the broad command of a criminal statute; but just as possibly the underlying statutory prohibition, whether enforceable by injunction or by criminal sanctions, may have a deterrent effect not varying with the particular sanction employed. It is said, moreover, that there is a difference in the time at which the offense is passed upon, that in the case of prior restraint the offense is judged prospectively, while in the case of criminal sanctions it is judged after it has been committed. But the judicial sanction takes its bite after the fact in either case, whether the sanction be fine or imprisonment for criminal violation or fine or imprisonment for violation of an injunctive or administrative order. In either case the facts of the violation are spread before a judicial tribunal after the event. And where the injunction relates to a specific publication, there is all the more warning to the defendant.

Is there then no validity in the conventional contrast between prior restraint and subsequent penalty? Several possible differences do exist. In the first place, the identity of the trier of fact is important. There are two sets of facts to be judged: what may be called facts of coverage (including interpretation and application of the governing standards), and facts of violation. Under an outright criminal law the two coalesce into one stage, determined ordinarily by a jury and at all events according to criminal procedure. Under a licensing or injunctive scheme the one determination is made by an administrative official or by a judge, with review normally by a judge, and the other determination is made by a judge in contempt proceedings or by the processes of criminal law. To the extent that an advisory jury is used by a court at the injunctive stage, the difference between this procedure and the outright criminal sanction on the score of the trier of fact is minimized.

Second, there may be a difference in the clarity and definiteness of the prohibition. On this point, however, no generalization is possible. The injunctive order may in fact be just as clear and definite as a penal statute, particularly if the order is issued with respect to a designated publication. Indeed, an injunctive order in some circumstances may afford greater guidance than a penal statute. Consider, for example, the case of *Valentine v. Chrestensen.*[35] An ordinance forbade the distribution of "commercial" handbills on the streets. The problem facing the prospective distributor was whether a handbill containing commercial matter on one side and matter of general noncommercial interest on the other could be distributed with impunity. The question might be determined in three ways. There might be, in the first place, a criminal prosecution after the event, in which case the distributor would have taken the risk of an erroneous construction. There might be, in the second place, an injunction against distribution. In that case the order would clarify the law before its pinch was felt, and the question could be finally resolved without the risk of punishment for an erroneous prophecy. There might be, in the third place, an injunction by the distributor against criminal prosecution, if a court of equity were willing to assume this jurisdiction. In such a case if the distributor should win, he would be protected as he would be under the second alternative. If he should lose, he would have the same authoritative notice with respect to future distribution, but the question of interim violations would remain. If his constitutional challenge were a reasonable one, though finally rejected, might it not be possible to enjoin prosecutions for the interim violations in the interest of removing a clog on the process of constitutional adjudication? Something of the kind has been done where a public utility has no means of challenging an order other than violation and exposure to multiple penalties.[36] Of course the utility is under a duty to serve, and it may be required to given bond to restore the status quo as a condition of avoiding prosecution for the interim violations. The case of the distributor of leaflets is relegated to a lower level unless it is recognized that the device of a bond to restore the status quo is impractical and that the duty to serve may find an equivalent in the public interest in freedom of expression in marginal cases while the validity of a restraint is being tested. At all events, the double standard here seems to operate in favor of the economic interest unless some such parallel comes to be drawn.

A third difference between prior restraint and subsequent punishment is suggested by this problem of interim violations. Suppose that the individual offender, rather than ultimately losing, eventually prevails on a full hearing of the constitutional issues. In a criminal trial he would of course suffer no punishment. In an injunctive or administrative proceeding, where a restraining order or temporary injunction has been issued against him or a permit withheld, but where a final injunction is ultimately denied or a permit granted, there is the serious problem of penalties for interim violations. If disobedience of the interim order is *ipso facto* contempt, with no opportunity to escape by showing the invalidity of the order on the merits, the restraint does indeed have a chilling effect beyond that of a criminal statute. To the extent, however, that local procedure allows such a defense to be raised in a contempt proceeding,[37] the special objection to prior restraint growing out of the problem of interim activity is obviated.

Where the prior restraint takes the form of administrative censorship, special objections arise. Historically the paradigm case of prior restraint was the English practice of the licensing of books and plays, with no provision for judicial review. Modern American practice does mitigate the evils of its historic prototype by furnishing an opportunity for review of the censor's orders in court; but the licensing system still entails features that ought to set it apart as peculiarly obnoxious to the guarantee of freedom of speech and press. Not only is the basic decision made by an official whose preoccupation is with a ban on publication; his order is the law unless and until the publisher shoulders the burden of going to court to overturn it. The force of inertia is put on the side of the censor.

In the movie-censorship case decided in 1960, these considerations were given too little attention. In upholding the Chicago censorship law, the majority of the Court addressed itself mainly to the argument of counsel for the exhibitor that the First Amendment guarantees at least one publication or exhibition before the law may intervene. This conception of the principle condemning prior restraint is a patently trivial one and merited no more than the answer of the Court. But the more realistic aspects of the problem, centering on the burden placed on the exhibitor, deserved more sympathetic attention.

The majority relied on a decision upholding the New York obscenity law, which provides for an injunction against the sale of an obscene publication; this, the majority pointed out, had been accepted over the protest of a minority who condemned it as a prior restraint.[38] But, as Chief Justice Warren pointed out in his dissent in the Chicago case, the two cases are quite different in significant procedural aspects: the burden of going to court, the burden of proof, the force of inertia, the element of delay in publication. Perhaps one can say of the decision that the minority had cried prior restraint so indiscriminately in earlier cases that the majority became desensitized to the creature when it actually appeared. Something similar has happened, I suggested in the preceding chapter, with respect to the clear-and-present-danger test.

In sum, it will hardly do to place all "prior restraint" in a special category for absolute condemnation. What is needed is a pragmatic assessment of its operation in the particular circumstances. The generalization that prior restraint is particularly obnoxious in civil liberties cases must yield to more particularistic analysis.

A comparable analysis needs to be made in assessing the proposition that a law regulating freedoms guaranteed by the First Amendment is to be judged "on its face." This proposition is on its own face at odds with the established rule that one who challenges a statute must show that it is unconstitutional as applied to him and the circumstances of his case. A departure in civil liberties cases may be thought to derive from the *Thornhill* decision,[39] where the new and special doctrine was announced by Mr. Justice Murphy. No separate opinions were delivered. Nevertheless the pronouncement that statutes interfering with freedom of speech are to be judged on their face was unnecessary to the decision, since so far as appears the picketing in which the defendants were engaged was peaceful picketing of a kind that was itself entitled to constitutional protection. It was therefore unnecessary to consider whether, had the picketing been of another kind, the defendants might still have escaped conviction because the statute made no differentiation in the breadth of its ban.

The problem of an overbroad statute, whether in the field of civil liberties or elsewhere, is really a special case of the problem of vagueness. A statute that is vague and indefinite—that prohibits, for example, "unreasonable prices"—is of course insupportable unless what is indefinite is made definite in advance by authoritative construction.[40] Essentially the same vice inheres in a statute that is overbroad. The terms themselves are not vague; a ban on all picketing is superficially precise. Yet the clarity of its language is delusive, since it will have to be recast in order to separate the constitutional from the unconstitutional applications. If it is read as applicable only where constitutionally so, the reading uncovers the vagueness that is latent in its terms.

The problem, as has been said, is not peculiar to civil liberties cases. A federal statute making it an offense to commit any act that is constitutionally punishable by the national government would presumably be invalid. Indeed, there was substantial doubt about the validity of a civil rights law punishing the deprivation of rights secured by the Constitution, insofar as it was sought to be applied to the evolving rights under the Fourteenth Amendment, even though the conduct of the defendant, a local sheriff, was so immoral as to constitute homicide.[41] In applying the rule against vagueness or overbroadness something, however, should depend on the moral quality of the conduct. In order not to chill conduct within the protection of the Constitution and having a genuine social utility, it may be necessary to throw the mantle of protection beyond the constitutional periphery, where the statute does not make the boundary clear. The public interest in freedom of expression may serve to invalidate an overbroad statute that casts a cloud on expression both within and without the constitutional boundary.

Can an overbroad statute be saved by construction? If the limiting construction is a relatively simple and natural one, it can probably be made to save the statute. A law requiring street parades to be licensed, but containing no standards to govern the grant of a license, appears to be invalid on its face, and yet when the highest court of the state interpreted it to condition the grant or refusal of a license only on the basis of safety and convenience of traffic, the Supreme Court accepted the limitation and sustained a conviction.[42] If, however, the terms are more at large, and if the true vice in such a case is, as suggested, latent vagueness, it is difficult to see how it can be cured in a given case by a construction in that very case placing valid limits on the statute. The objection of vagueness is twofold: inadequate guidance to the individual whose conduct is regulated, and inadequate guidance to the triers of fact.[43] The former objection could not be cured retrospectively by a ruling either of the trial court or the appellate court, though it might be cured for the future by an authoritative judicial gloss. The latter objection—inadequate guidance to the triers of fact—might be cured by appropriate instructions at the trial stage or on remand under directions from the appellate court.

This analysis of the so-called *Thornhill* doctrine, it must be acknowledged, has not appeared to guide the Court in its treatment of the problem of statutes "void on their face." Despite the *Thornhill* opinion, the Court on occasion has remanded a case to the state court for clarification of a statute involving a regulation of civil liberties, and has also considered such a statute in terms of its narrowed construction by the appellate court of the state in the very case.[44]

The canons concerning "prior restraint" on speech and statutes "void on their face" are at the center of the controversy over the right of neo-Nazis to be given permits to speak in public places. Three cases decided by the Court on the same day in 1951 may serve, by a process of triangulation, to mark out more clearly the proper constitutional standards. One case, *Niemotko v. Maryland*,[45] presented prior restraint in its baldest form. The city council of Havre de Grace, Maryland, heard an application of Jehovah's Witnesses to use a public park at a stated time for the purpose of conducting a

Bible talk. Without benefit of any ordinance laying down standards of discretion, and apparently without any explicit basis for the determination, the city council denied the request. Upon commencement of the meeting without a permit the speaker was arrested, and he was later convicted on a charge of disorderly conduct. The Supreme Court was unanimous in reversing the judgment of conviction. There is nothing surprising about the case except the fact that the Court of Appeals of Maryland had declined to review the conviction on the ground that the issues were not "matters of public interest."

At the opposite pole is the case of *Feiner v. New York*.[46] There was involved here no licensing or permit practice or injunctive procedure. The petitioner was convicted of disorderly conduct under the New York penal laws. He had spoken on a sidewalk in Syracuse to a crowd of seventy-five or eighty people made up of Negroes and white persons who overflowed the sidewalk into the street. His voice was carried through a loud speaker; he was urging his listeners to attend a meeting sponsored by the Young Progressives and in the course of the speech used derogatory but not profane language with reference to the city authorities, President Truman, and the American Legion. He urged his listeners to rise up and fight for their rights. Whether he urged them to "rise up in arms" was a matter of some uncertainty in the record, but the lower courts so found. The crowd became restless, there was some movement and excitement in the crowd, a police officer was asked to take action, and after he had requested the petitioner to come down from the speaker's box several times over a space of four or five minutes he arrested the petitioner, who had been talking for half an hour. The conviction was affirmed by the Supreme Court, but not unanimously. Justices Black, Douglas, and Minton dissented.

The third and intermediate case, *Kunz v. New York*,[47]

is the most difficult of the three and presents some complexities in the problem of prior restraint. The appellant had been granted a permit in 1946 under an ordinance permitting a clergyman to conduct religious services in public places but making it unlawful for any person "to ridicule or denounce any form of religious belief." In November 1946 his permit was revoked after a hearing by the police commissioner; the revocation was based on evidence that he had ridiculed and denounced religious beliefs of others in his meetings. In 1947 and 1948 appellant was refused a permit, and upon his speaking without a permit at Columbus Circle in New York City he was arrested. He was charged with holding a meeting for public worship without a permit, he was convicted, and the conviction was affirmed by a four-to-three decision of the New York Court of Appeals. The Supreme Court reversed the conviction, Mr. Justice Jackson dissenting.

The precise scope of the decision is not entirely clear from the opinion of the Court delivered by Chief Justice Vinson. In particular, it is not clear whether a prior restraint, at least where it is not based on considerations of time and place, is *ipso facto* invalid. At one point the Chief Justice states: "We have here, then, an ordinance which gives an administrative official discretionary power to control in advance the right of citizens to speak on religious matters on the streets of New York. As such, the ordinance is clearly invalid as a prior restraint on the exercise of First Amendment rights." [48] At the close of the opinion a somewhat narrower formulation is announced: "It is sufficient to say that New York cannot vest restraining control over the right to speak on religious subjects in an administrative official where there are no appropriate standards to guide his action." [49] On the facts of the case, it will be observed, neither the revocation of the permit nor the refusal to grant a new one was based on any express standards in the ordinance. Apparently the ordinance was construed to authorize revocation where the permit holder did in fact denounce or ridicule a form of religious belief. If a further step in construction could be taken and the ordinance interpreted to authorize withholding of a permit where such conduct had previously or recently occurred on the part of the applicant, there would remain the serious question whether such a standard is adequate as a basis for suppressing speech in a public place. It appeared in fact that the appellant prior to the revocation had used inflammatory language of a kind calculated to arouse disorderly conduct on the part of admirers as well as of the objects of the abuse. It is in reliance on that evidence that Mr. Justice Jackson would have affirmed the conviction. He regards the opinion of the majority as holding that such speeches "are within [appellant's] constitutional freedom and therefore New York City has no power to require a permit." [50] And again: "This Court today initiates the doctrine that language such as this, in the environment of the street meeting, is immune from prior municipal control." [51] Quite possibly Mr. Justice Jackson gives too much breadth to the prevailing opinion. In any event, it is hard to follow his conclusion that the facts disclosed in 1946 sustain a denial of a permit in 1948 where the hearing on the application in the latter year was not focused by any provision of the ordinance, or by any settled construction, on the issue of the likelihood that the applicant would engage in insulting and abusive talk calculated to stir his hearers to breaches of the peace. Surely we can demand as much direction in an ordinance of this kind as in a statute providing for jurisdiction over nonresidents, where, it has been held, the fact that nonresidents actually received notice does not cure a statute that fails to provide an orderly procedure for giving the notice.[52]

The separate opinion of Mr. Justice Frankfurter, concurring in the result in all three cases, makes it clear that he will not follow any absolute dogma regarding the invalidity of prior restraint. In his judgment the vice in the conviction was that the relevance of the prior facts to the denial of a permit was not defined in advance. In his view the nub of the case was this:

> In the present case, Kunz was not arrested for what he said on the night of arrest, nor because at that time he was disturbing the peace or interfering with traffic. He was arrested because he spoke without a license, and the license was refused because the police commissioner thought it likely on the basis of past performance that Kunz would outrage the religious sensibilities of others. If such had been the supportable finding on the basis of fair standards in safeguarding peace in one of the most populous centers of New York City, this Court would not be justified in upsetting it. It would not be censorship in advance. . . . The situation here disclosed is not, to reiterate, beyond control on the basis of regulation appropriately directed to the evil.[53]

In order to suggest the artificiality of an absolute distinction between prior restraint and subsequent punishment, the following case may serve. Suppose that Kunz had been prosecuted and convicted for breach of the peace in 1946 under the statute and upon facts that were held to support Feiner's conviction. Suppose further that a sentence of thirty days in jail was imposed, but execution suspended on condition that the defendant not engage in street meetings during that period. Would such a condition be unconstitutional as a prior restraint? Perhaps this illustration, in its application to the more general problem of prior restraint, is an attempt to prove the unknown by means of the more unknown—what the logicians call *ignotum per ignotius*. In any event, the use of recent prior misconduct as a gound for enjoining street meetings for a limited future time raises issues comparable to those that have been encountered in the enjoining of picketing where there has been a record of recent violence on the part of the picketers.[54] It need hardly be added that the discussion is in terms of constitutional limits, not necessarily of the wisest method for the localities to adopt within their constitutional power.

It is to be hoped that future cases will not be solved by a facile application of the subsequent-punishment—prior-restraint dichotomy. An order not to circulate a specific publication is different from an order forbidding circulation of a publication not yet composed. An order indefinitely suppressing future issues is different from an order limited in time and coverage. An order forbidding the circulation of a periodical differs from an order forbidding a street meeting. An order forbidding a street meeting because of its sponsorship is different from one forbidding such a meeting because of recently punished or possibly even punishable conduct by the speaker on similar occasions. A law defining appropriate standards governing permits differs from a law that leaves the local authorities at large to find grounds for a denial. If the *Kunz* case is interpreted in this light, the three decisions taken together will go far to bring greater clarity and order in a field where guidance is needed by speakers, local public officials, and the courts.

In all these cases the Court is called on to weigh the claims of public order and the exhortations of the nonconformist. The task unfortunately cannot be performed by any mechanical device for testing the centripetal and centrifugal forces in our community. For the Court the problem is the fearful one of so measuring the tensions, or so reviewing the measurements made by others, as not to appear absurd in the sight of history.[55]

## II. *A Double Standard in Principle*

At the threshold of the development that was to bring liberty of speech within the purview of the Fourteenth Amendment a commentator was moved to ask whether the philosophy of judicial tolerance to state social and economic legislation should not also embrace state restrictions on liberty of speech:

> Courts are upholding such "social" legislation with increasing sympathy, which is what we wish them to do. The majority opinion in *Lochner v. New York*, the New York bakers' case, seems a long way off. But will not the same kind of argument and the same line of thought which upholds a law which restricts a man in the contracts he may make, or limits him in the use to which he may lawfully put his real estate, uphold a law limiting the exercise of his tongue when the majority so wills it? [56]

A quarter of a century later Judge Learned Hand, in a passage quoted in the preceding chapter, found it appropriate to commend the late Chief Justice Stone for his resistance to a current of thought that would sweep away, through judicial review, controls on one kind of liberty while leaving almost unimpaired controls on other kinds.

Is there any ground in reason for treating differently experiments in social and economic legislation and experiments in the control of speech and assembly and religious observances? Judge Hand has done a service in reminding us that these problems as they come before a court do not present a clash of absolutes; legislation, whether it restrains freedom to hire or freedom to speak, is itself an effort at compromise between the claims of the social order and individual freedom, and when the legislative compromise in either case is brought to the judicial test the court stands one step removed from the conflict and its resolution through law. The question of the preferred position of First Amendment freedoms cannot, however, be so easily disposed of. Mr. Justice Frankfurter is right in cautioning against the epithet "preferred position" for those freedoms if the epithet threatens to become a substitute for analysis.[57] And yet there are issues here of political philosophy which should be reconnoitered. For the subject is, like a castle of the mind, not to be encompassed by a single fervent assault or taken by a trumpet blast, still less by tooting one horn of a dilemma.

Textual arguments to support a preferred position for one set of liberties have been reviewed in the preceding chapter and found unsatisfying. Historical arguments, too, are inconclusive, in light of the marked strain of dedication to rights of property in our heritage. Indeed, reliance on the validation of history for a valuation of guarantees puts more weight on history than it can safely bear. There is, in the first place, an element of question begging in the process if we start by seeking those warranties most essential for a "free society." Our findings might be different if we described our end as a stable or a prosperous society. More important than this, history as a guide to the priority of values becomes the creative art of the historian. If the history we learn comes to us from Whig historians, as Professor Butterfield has reminded us, it behooves us to inquire why this view of history holds for us its special attraction. Santayana has spoken of an "estimate of evolution" as "a sort of retrospective politics," engaged in as one "might look over a crowd to find his friends." [58] From Lord Acton came a similar warning against confounding the historian with the history:

> Whatever a man's notions of these later centuries are, such, in the main, the man himself will be. Under the name of History, they cover the articles of his philosophic, his religious and his political creed. They give his measure, they denote his character: and, as praise is the shipwreck of historians, his preferences betray him more than his aversions. Modern history touches us so nearly, it is so deep a question of life and death, that we are bound to find our way through it, and to owe our insight to ourselves.[59]

History, to be sure, can show us a number of things. It can show us specific events: that, for example, the

Habeas Corpus Act of 1679, so far from being the fountainhead of personal liberty, simply made some liberalizing changes in existing practice; or that the expiration in 1695 of the laws on licensing of the press was not accompanied by ringing affirmations of the principle of free speech but was allowed to come about because the system of licensing had entailed too many administrative problems. History may perform a somewhat broader service. It can give us a narrative; it can tell us, for example, with a little luck in finding the sources, what was the practice regarding jury trial for contempt in the centuries preceding our Constitution. And finally, without subscribing to the idea that sociology is history with the history left out, one can acknowledge the important potentialities of history as a source of data on the limitations of institutional arrangements with respect to achieving their goals. But, to recur, all of this instructiveness is quite short of yielding judgments about the priority of values. The great landmarks of liberty under law are identified as such by generations whose concerns, needs, and aspirations are reflected in their historians. Under the sheep's covering of history lies the lion's skin of philosophy. Confronted with an ultimate choice of warrants, the libertarian is not likely to hesitate. Would it really matter, for example, if a historian argued persuasively that English literature had its greatest flowering in a period of the licensing of books and plays; or, more broadly, that artistic and religious vitality have been most marked under the pressure of suppressive laws moderately enforced?

It is time to pass from textual and historical arguments to some philosophical approaches to the problem of the double standard.

*Natural rights.* There are those who would start with the proposition that self-expression is the distinctive vocation of mankind and is therefore to be preferred over all other freedoms. In nothing is man so much himself as in the enterprise of communicating, inquiring, and debating.

For judges there is an obvious danger in casting about for natural rights and determining which are more "natural" than others. The making of a will, for example, has at times been regarded as a "natural right"—a view that produces complications when a legislature imposes an estate tax or limits the freedom of choice of a testator. Moreover, a concept as protean as property is an unsafe foundation on which to construct a legally responsible system of natural rights. To Locke, to whom we owe the "life, liberty, and property" of the Constitution, the idea of property was doubtless an extension of the human personality, comprising the fruits of one's labor, the tools of one's trade, and the household goods and lands with which one was surrounded. Property consisted of "belongings" in an intimate sense. Today property has been largely dehumanized. Much of it is owned by corporate aggregates, expressively called by the French *sociétés anonymes*. The property of individuals has more and more come to consist of the value of relationships to groups to which the individuals belong, whether as investors or as workers. Property still represents "belongings," but in another sense. This transformation could hardly have come about without the assistance of the courts. Could the courts be expected to differentiate, in the name of the Constitution, between one kind of emerging property claim and another? As in the case of attachment or bankruptcy laws, the state may give special protection to a homestead and to working tools, but it would be difficult and dangerous for judges to find warrant for requiring such priorities in the broad guaranties of the Constitution.

Related to the doctrine of natural rights is the view that certain freedoms are basic preconditions for others. "Freedom of expression," Mr. Justice Cardozo declared, "is the matrix, the indispensable condition, of nearly every other form of freedom." [60] And yet a strong case can be made for the proposition that minimal material provision is the truly basic condition for human liberty. To exercise choice as a moral being presupposes some actuality of alternatives. Long ago, in dealing with the liberty of contract, lawyers recognized that "a necessitous man is not a free man." The making of positive provision for material security is thus a vital guide to political and legislative action; but courts, in applying constitutional guaranties, cannot bestow such security. Many of the newer constitutions in all parts of the globe enumerate among fundamental human rights the right to work, to assistance in time of illness, and to security in old age; but these are put as moral incentives to legislation, not as judicially enforceable constitutional rights.

*Useful spontaneity.* Those who find in the freedom of the market for goods a prototype for other freedoms are likely to adopt as a governing criterion the test whether spontaneity or superimposed planning, individual choices or central control, will produce the most serviceable results in a given undertaking. Is the enterprise one like solving a jigsaw puzzle (to take an illustration from Michael Polanyi's *Logic of Liberty*) or like assembling a Chevrolet? In the former category might be put such activities as pamphleteering, stock-market trading, and legal counseling; in the latter category, street parades, the erection of water-power dams, and naval maneuvers. More meaningful, however, than classifying activities is to distinguish between the several kinds of controls that may be employed. Which restraints serve to maximize liberty; which of them are, in the words of the Harvard commencement citation for the LL.B. degree, "those wise restraints which make men free"? Does a resale-price-maintenance law, which enhances the liberty of manufacturers by broadening the effect of their contracts, while curtailing the liberty of nonassenting retailers, work in the direction of greater or lesser economic freedom? Does a public-utility holding-company act, which contributes to the understanding and effective choice of investors while limiting the discretion (or indiscretion) of corporate managers, augment or curtail human freedom? This kind of calculus, which is a commonplace of the legislative process, raises philosophical and practical problems of the first importance. The question for us is whether the calculus is an appropriate one for the jurisdiction of judges in applying the guaranties of the Constitution. The experience of the judicial veto in the first two decades of this century argues strongly against this kind of role for judges in passing on the validity of legislation. It would be but a short step from the *Social Statics* of Herbert Spencer to the social ecstatics of the judges.

*Skepticism.* A different philosophic grounding for freedom of expression is found in the skepticism of Mr. Justice Holmes. The witticism that "the best test of truth is the power of the thought to get itself accepted in the competition of the market" [61] has brought down on Holmes the heavy thunder of the critics of a natural law persuasion. These critics perhaps make too little allowance for Holmes's jaunty irreverence of speech, his astringent washing-down of flabby moralizing, his delight in shocking the legal bourgeoisie. On occasion, however, he so far forgot his manners as to speak solemnly of freedom of speech and press as "very sacred rights." [62] Like all skeptical philosophies, Holmes's would be self-defeating in the end if carried to what he would have called a drily logical extreme. For if no idea is essentially more deserving of respect than another, a legislature might well adopt the idea of censorship until a different doctrine came to prevail. Holmes's philosophy, in other words, requires amplification in its concept of the competition of the market: it must recognize that the market is to be kept open, with suitable procedures for self-correction, as in the case of the scientific process. The skepticism of Holmes himself was tempered by a romantic faith in heroic action: he was an existentialist before existentialism. However undeveloped his philosophy may have been, his skepticism does at least furnish a pragmatic basis for distinguishing experimentation in the control of ideas from experimentation in the control of physical and economic activity. We can be surer of our aim and the propriety of the means when we deal with food and drugs or even their prices than when we deal with the "poison" of ideas. Official censorship draws a parallel between material and mental poison, between violence to the body and to the spirit. But it would be dangerous to forget that we are here dealing in metaphors.

*Representative self-government.* The standards that have been canvassed thus far are useful as philosophical and political guides for the framing and the critique of legislation. They are less suited, I have suggested, as criteria for judges in applying constitutional guaranties, because they involve the positive furnishing of wherewithal, or they require judgments that judges are not especially competent or chosen to make and that as constitutional glosses would be virtually irreversible. The standard of representative self-government is, however, more promising.

This criterion, deriving from Mill's linkage of freedom of expression with the self-improvement of a mature society, has been most cogently developed by Dr. Alexander Meiklejohn, who in his volume *Free Speech* reminds us that it is the "mutilation of the thinking process of the community" from which the First Amendment was designed to save us.[63] The right to speak is the individualized legal reflection of the more generalized right to hear, which is basic to the process of political flux.

There is here, I believe, a useful analogue in the market place for goods, but the analogue is not the local market. Rather it is the concept of a national market, which no state can freely foreclose because the market involves outside interests that are not represented within the state. It is the federal system in the commercial realm which provides a parallel to the control of expression by the state, and the key is the concept of representation. In the realm of ideas, hearers may not freely be foreclosed; although they are represented in such a political effort, the representation is *ultra vires*, so to speak, for a minority cannot with ordinary latitude delegate to a majority the control of the flow of ideas. The decision whether or not to listen or attend is not as delegable as the decision whether to license a new electric utility. Is not this the meaning of the Supreme Court's ruling in the doorbell ringing case? The Court held that a municipal ordinance may not prohibit religious evangelists from traveling from door to door, even though the city fathers valued privacy above the message of the intruders.[64] It was left for each householder, under the Court's decision, to decide for himself whether to receive the messengers or to make them trespassers by posting a warning sign. No compact majority could act for all potential hearers, any more than one state can set a rule for others in the regulation of interstate commerce.

To base fundamental freedoms on this principle of representative self-government fortunately avoids any commitment to theories of truth or any alliance with schools of skepticism or belief. Consequently we can temper the storm raised by the natural-law philosophers over the skepticism of Mr. Justice Holmes. The consensus that is required is only an agreement on secular, political principles: that in a political community a citizen is an end, not a means; that pluralistic centers of interest and power treated with fraternal respect and even-handedly, are, in the end, a fostering source of a healthy sense of community; that, as Madison long ago foresaw, a tyranny of the majority is forestalled when the majority itself is a shifting consensus of minorities.

That this political philosophy is consistent with a self-confident orthodoxy in matters of belief is the teaching of thoughtful religious spokesmen. Let me quote two passages to document the point. The first is from Reinhold Niebuhr's *The Children of Light and the Children of Darkness*. Dr. Niebuhr is speaking of moral truths and their inevitable historical corruptions and misappropriations and partial formulations. "This alone," he asserts, "would justify the ultimate freedom of a democratic society, in which not even the moral presuppositions upon which the society rests are withdrawn from constant scrutiny and reexamination. Only through such freedom can the premature arrest of new vitalities in history be prevented. . . . A society which exempts ultimate principles from criticism will find difficulty in dealing with the historical forces which have appropriated these truths as their special possession."[65]

As a second exhibit I offer an editorial from *The Pilot*, publication of the Catholic Archdiocese of Boston, commenting on the Supreme Court's decision striking down the New York ban on the motion picture *The Miracle:*

> For some strange reason the impression has got about that Catholics are uniformly unhappy about the recent ruling of the Supreme Court on the occasion of "The Miracle" case. This simply is not so. The unanimous decision of the Court had nothing to say about the grossly insulting nature of the film or its sacrilegious character, and those who found it offensive artistically and religiously can continue to hold their views. Similarly those who wish to boycott it and persuade others to do the same have no reason to desist.
>
> The Supreme Court merely indicated its incapacity to define an essentially theological term—*sacrilegious*.

> No one should be surprised that a group of jurists exercising a civil function in a pluralistic society should refrain from such a definition. This is not to say that the word is indefinable; Catholics have very clear notions on the meaning of sacrilege, so too, more or less, have the two-hundred-odd Christian sects in America. Even those religions which are non-Christian have a definition of sacrilege.
>
> We are faced with the question of the function of the state in a society where various religions are conscientiously held by their adherents. The civil power must protect the consciences of its citizens in those matters which do not damage the general welfare; it will scarcely do for the civil authorities however to determine what is sacred, or what is sacrilegious. When they speak in these accents they assume a competence which is not theirs."[66]

These statements carry a reminder that our tradition of civil liberty rests not only on the secularism of a Thomas Jefferson but also on the fervent sectarianism (as Perry Miller has shown) of a Roger Williams.[67]

When we turn to the problem of *limitations* on freedom of expression and association, which after all is the crucial issue, the philosophers give us dismayingly little guidance. Consider the advice of the classic philosophers of liberty of speech, the great secular trinity of Johns—Milton, Locke, and Mill.

In the *Areopagitica* Milton places certain kinds of self-expression out of bounds: "I mean not tolerated popery, and open supersitition, which, as it extirpates all religious and civil supremacies, so itself should be extirpate, provided first that all charitable and compassionate means be used to win and regain the weak and the misled; that also which is impious or evil absolutely either against faith or manners no law can possibly permit, that intends not to unlaw itself." Interesting as this pronouncement is in the history of ideas, and revealing as it is of the English mind's drawing-back from what it regards as the excesses of its logic, its specific advice will hardly be found helpful in twentieth-century America.

If we consult Locke's *Letter Concerning Toleration*, we find another group of outcasts marked off again by religion: ". . . those are not at all to be tolerated who deny the being of God. Promises, covenants, and oaths, which are the bonds of human society, can have no hold upon an atheist." There are ironic lessons to be learned from this passage for our day, unintended by Locke, regarding the value of classification of individuals according to a psychology of groups; but the explicit advice on toleration is scarcely more tolerable than Milton's.

Still another exclusion is made by Mill in his essay *On Liberty:* "Liberty, as a principle, has no application to any state of things anterior to the time when mankind have become capable of being improved by free and equal discussion. Until then, there is nothing for them but implicit obedience to an Akbar or a Charlemagne, if they are so fortunate as to find one." This passage reflects Mill's fruitful idea that freedom of expression is a corollary of self-government, but it is put in a way that might lead to a prolongation of tutelage or paternalistic censorship. Mill's antagonist, Sir James Stephen, was quick to seize the opening, in his *Liberty, Equality, Fraternity:* "Why then may not educated men coerce the ignorant? What is there in the character of a very commonplace ignorant peasant or petty shopkeeper in these days which makes him a less fit subject for coercion on Mr. Mill's principle than the Hindoo nobles and princes who were coerced by Akbar?"

For our purposes, it seems to me, the most useful reference point for limitations on fundamental freedoms is to be found by recurring to the analogy of the free national market safeguarded against local self-interest. In the early nineteenth century the Court strove to reach decisions in this field by classifying state laws as regulations of commerce (and so invalid) on the one hand, or regulations of local health and safety (and so valid) on the other. But, to take a homely example, how does one classify a state law requiring that all milk sold locally must be pasteurized under the supervision of the authorities of the consuming state? This is surely a health measure, and if only local commercial interests were involved, it would certainly be a valid regulation, consistent with due process of law. The problem arises because when applied to milk transported from another state the measure is *both* a regulation of health and a regulation of commerce; and the Court reached the beginning of wisdom when it treated such cases accordingly, recognizing that they presented issues of more or less, of the importance of the local interest as weighed against the burden on commerce and the availability of other, less drastic means to achieve the local end without a corresponding burden on the multistate market.

The same sort of approach is fruitful for cases of fundamental freedoms. Consider, for example, the problem of group libel laws.[68] By some judges group libel is thought to be no more than eighteenth-century pamphleteering or coffeehouse talk, immune from any sort of governmental restraint. By other judges it is regarded as simply another kind of libel, subject to all the governmental control that we accept in the case of defamation of individuals. Only when it is recognized that group libel partakes of both categories can we develop workable standards of judicial review. These might include such factors as specific intent to incite to violence, the defense of truth, and clear and present danger—the imminence of the danger, its relative seriousness (Is it littering of streets or race riots?), and the availability of other protective measures less suppressive of public speech (penalties for conspiracy to overthrow the government or to teach covertly espionage or sabotage). This kind of analysis is closely akin to that which the Court has applied quite successfully, on the whole, in the field of state regulation of interstate commerce.

If this makes of the Court a kind of super-city-council, I see no escape, unless the Court is to revert to illusory absolutes. The issues thus viewed, it is worth emphasizing, are unlike those of the era of judicial vetoes of economic legislation. There, certain kinds of activity were held utterly immune—men's hours of labor, wages, and prices, except for businesses "affected with a public interest." The analogy to the commerce cases, on the other hand, means that governments may do things in a right way and not in a wrong—a disproportionately repressive—way. If the Court does require a local government to turn square corners when it deals with interstate commerce or trade in ideas, it is vindicating its responsibility as the guardian of structure and process.

## III. *Effectiveness of Judicial Review*

How effective is Supreme Court review in civil liberties cases? Once again Judge Learned Hand has posed the issue:

> And so to sum up, I believe that for by far the greater part of their work it is a condition upon the success of our system that the judges should be independent; and I do not believe that their independence should be impaired because of their constitutional function. But the price of this immunity, I insist, is that they should not have the last word in those basic conflicts of "right and wrong—between whose endless jar justice resides." You may ask what then will become of the fundamental principles of equity and fair play which our constitutions enshrine; and whether I seriously believe that unsupported they will serve merely as counsels of moderation. I do not think that anyone can say what will be left of those principles; I do not know whether they will serve only

> as counsels; but this much I think I do know—that a society so riven that the spirit of moderation is gone, no court *can* save; that a society where that spirit flourishes, no court *need* save; that in a society which evades its responsibility by thrusting upon courts the nurture of that spirit, that spirit in the end will perish.[69]

There is surely great strength in Judge Hand's position. Regeneration comes from within. The restraints that the Constitution forbids are, essentially, only those of public, not private, action. And when the Court has spoken resoundingly, the occasion calling for the vindication of civil liberties has often receded into history and the Court has only caught up with a new tide of sentiment. When, for example, the *Endo* decision was rendered in 1944, holding invalid the regulations governing evacuated Japanese, the federal authorities had announced on the preceding day the termination of the program of detention of loyal citizens of Japanese ancestry.[20] Furthermore, decisions vindicating civil liberties may lose much of their apparent force through evasion on the level of actual practice. While a racial covenant is not enforceable by a court against a willing seller and a willing buyer, there are signs that discriminatory practices of private lending institutions may make extremely difficult the purchase of property on mortgage where such a covenant or equivalent practice is in operation. While Negroes may not systematically be excluded from jury panels, it appears that counsel may exercise peremptory challenges to achieve the same result.[71] All of these considerations fortify Judge Hand's admonition against placing our trust in judicial enforcement of the Bill of Rights.

And yet there are heavy weights that must be placed on the other side of the scale. Judge Hand has put the dilemma of a people lost beyond redemption or healthy beyond the need of saving. In fact our situation falls between. The question is not whether the courts can do everything but whether they can do something. Moreover, the cleavage between growth from within and alteration imposed from without is not absolute. Education and the practice of self-improvement may be fostered by judicious judicial intervention. Decisions refusing enforcement of restrictive covenants and forbidding segregation in public education break down barriers that in the past have impeded the process of enlightenment through experience in living.

The Court, furthermore, does more than decide controversies and maintain a balance of governmental powers. It serves as a symbol, and particularly so in the area of civil liberties. When great classic utterances in this field are invoked, the English are apt to call upon Milton and Mill, while we are likely to summon up Holmes and Hughes and Brandeis. Jefferson apart, our preceptors in civil liberties have tended to be judges, whose opinions imponderably but surely influence our course of action far beyond the occasions that have called them forth. Of course the Court does not sit as a symbol or to compose for the anthologies. We accept the Court as a symbol in the measure that, while performing its appointed tasks, it manages at the same time to articulate and rationalize the aspirations reflected in the Constitution. We are able thus to achieve in some measure the legal guarantees of a Bill of Rights and the moral and intellectual qualities of a Declaration of Rights. Indeed, those qualities are vivified by the very necessity of concreteness and accommodation of principles in the test of specific controversy. It is rather idle to speculate whether it would have been better to leave the Bill of Rights virtually without judicial sanction. Conceivably we might have developed something like questions in the House of Commons as an effective substitute. But our history and habits have taken another course, and to conjecture on the responsibility and self-restraint of government had judicial review not been adopted is less hazardous than to estimate the consequence of a shift in practice after more than a century and a half of accommodation to the tradition of judicial sanctions.[72]

These considerations pro and con are relatively abstract and inconclusive. We need to know more than we do about the effect of judicial decisions on official conduct at the lowest operating level. We ought to encourage studies of the impact of decisions on the drafting of ordinances and regulations and on their administration. We do, however, have some evidence of a positive sort. Thus, after the decision in *Hague v. C.I.O.*[73] Jersey City revised its ordinance on permits for meetings in public places, producing a fair and carefully drawn plan.[74] No one can read the *Proceedings of the National Institute of Municipal Law Officers* without being made aware of the preoccupation of those officials with Supreme Court decisions and the problems of draftsmanship and enforcement which they raise. One of the activities of the group is the preparation and distribution of drafts of model ordinances. Significantly, two of these have related to municipal control of sound trucks and municipal control of comic books, subjects familiar to students of the *Supreme Court Reports.*[75]

This preoccupation with drafting and enforcement at the local level reflects the fact that Supreme Court decisions in this field deal not so much with absolute prohibitions as with questions of standards and methods. The infirmities are curable. Sound trucks may not be subjected to an unfettered licensing power, but may be controlled in respect of time and place and volume.[76] Jehovah's Witnesses may not be subjected to a license tax on the distribution and sale of their literature, but other forms of taxation, such as a net-income tax or a general-property tax, are presumably applicable.[77] The Witnesses may not be forbidden by ordinance to knock on doors, but presumably an ordinance may make it criminal to do so where the householder has posted a notice.[78] In actuality, therefore, these momentous constitutional cases frequently come down to such alternatives as whether the city fathers may place on receptive householders the burden of posting a welcome or must place on resistent householders the burden of posting a sign of inhospitality. The difference is by no means trivial, but it need not be inflated to the dimensions of irreconcilable principles. One may perhaps be forgiven for suggesting that if the cases were treated in this particularistic light, some of the acerbity in the divisions of the Court might be avoided. Mediation might be promoted if there were closer focus on areas of actual agreement; to stress the narrowness rather than the largeness of the issues dividing the Court would not be to lose sight of their significance.

# IV. UMPIRING THE FEDERAL SYSTEM

It is a commonplace that the great divisive contests in American history have been played out across the boards, as it were, of the Supreme Court. There, as in the sublimation of a morality play, have passed in review before a tribunal of authoritative critics the dramatic conflicts over slavery; the contest between land and water transportation; the struggle of industrial competition against the forces of concentration, the clashing interest of workers, consumers, and investors, and the claims of dissenting groups and individuals. A federal system presupposes diversity and must cope with corresponding tensions. Does it assume also a judiciary vested with the role of arbiter?

## I. *The Role of the Court*

The Anglo-American tradition has accustomed us to identifying with judges the task of constitutional arbitration. Elsewhere, however, the practice has not been standardized. The example of Switzerland reminds us that a federation, while entrusting review of state authority to a national judiciary, may reserve for the people the function of deciding whether a national law is consistent with the constitution. The French constitution of 1946 suggests another device that might be adapted to a federation; it establishes a Constitutional Committee, elected in part by the National Assembly at the beginning of each annual session, to which is confided the task of determining whether the laws passed by the National Assembly require amendment of the constitution. The contemporary Constitution of Yugoslavia, inverting the practice whereby a government may seek from the judiciary a constitutional decision, authorizes the Federal Supreme Court to apply to the Federal People's Assembly for a decision on the conformity of federal laws with the federal constitution.[1] Thus is the rule of law accommodated to the environment of this or that brand of democracy. In the United States the Senate might have been employed as an arbiter of constitutional disputes between states and nation, as Madison tentatively suggested,[2] but such a role would very probably have intensified the identification of the Senate with local interests. From this point of view an important function of the judiciary is to relieve the legislators of the task of resolving conflicts between local power and national concern—a task that might have been felt to call for a duty of insularity.

Even in the United States, however, the conflicts between localism and centralism are by no means resolved wholly by the apparatus of judicial review. It is part of our political theory that each department of the government has responsibility in the first instance for interpreting and applying the Constitution as a limitation on its own action. The President's use of the veto on constitutional grounds, if not overridden by Congress, will foreclose the courts from receiving the question of constitutional law. Congress, moreover, enjoys considerable authority over the jurisdiction of the federal courts, which it can exercise to cut off the appellate jurisdiction of the Supreme Court, as it did in the Reconstruction era,[3] or to place limits on the jurisdiction of the lower federal courts.[4]

Furthermore, in the area of interstate commercial relations Congress can overturn a judgment of the Court under the interstate commerce clause by announcing a judgment of its own on the question whether the subject requires uniformity of regulation, if any is undertaken, or permits diversity of treatment.[5] Similarly Congress can waive the immunity of its agencies from state taxation or may, within limits, confer an immunity that the courts would not by themselves have recognized.[6] The legislation following the decision on offshore oil deposits testifies to the assumed authority of Congress to yield to the states what in the judgment of the Court belonged to the nation.[7] Many an interstate bone of contention is amicably divided under compacts between the states with the assent of Congress—in lieu of submission to the process of litigation. And in the crucial area of fiscal relations the leverage exerted by a federal grant-in-aid or a federal tax mitigated by a conditional credit may determine the balance of state and national functions and promote a degree of uniformity quite outside the framework of the judicial process. While the Court may be called upon to pass on the scheme's legitimacy, the particular provisions of the plan will be determined by political forces responding to economic pressures, whether in matters of inheritance taxation or unemployment insurance or loans and grants for municipal hydroelectric plants.[8] The overwhelming effect of the federal taxing power and its supremacy is pointed up by the recent experience of Australia and to some extent of Canada, where federal-state fiscal relations have resolved themselves into round-table bargaining for federal funds.[9] Although this experience has been less extreme with us, it does point to at least a potential truth in the observation of Karl Loewenstein that "A state with a federal income tax is no longer a genuinely federal state." [10]

The role of the judiciary is limited not only by the resourcefulness of other branches of government but also by the complexes of private power that lie outside the framework of constitutional limitations. Whether we are to enjoy a free national market, as the commerce clause envisaged, depends as much upon the practices of business enterprise as upon the governmental acts of member states. While a state may not by legislative fiat permit its commercial resources to be developed for local enjoyment and forbid their export to other states,[11] the Constitution is silent and neutral on the power of private groups thus to restrict the market. The Constitution reflects an eighteenth-century faith in economic liberalism. In this sense Professor Loewenstein is right in stating: "Federalism is a product of liberal thinking. It applied the (relative) freedom of the individual to the (relative) freedom of organization of territorial entities. It thrives as long as a free economy thrives. Speaking again sententiously: Economic planning is the DDT of federalism." [12]

But this is only to say that economic relations are in large part outside the province of those self-executing constitutional mandates that can be enforced solely through judicial control. These relations are remitted to the legislative power, so that the Sherman Act has become as important to the maintenance of the free national market as the commerce clause. Moreover, the implication that economic control is synonymous with centralization is not quite true. In more than one segment of the economy we have employed the resources of co-operative federalism to integrate local planning with national policy. The federal "hot oil" statute, which forbids the interstate shipment of oil produced in excess of state quotas is an example;[13] another is the federal assistance given to the state-controlled marketing of the raisin crop in California.[14] Our concern with these devices is that, once the general pattern is validated by the Court, the structure and balance of forces, both private and public, that shape the federal system are left to the working of politics. Thus the courts may be conceived as umpires determining what kinds of contests are permissible, leaving the choice of contests and the detailed rules to be worked out by the immediate participants.

With these qualifications in mind we turn to the experience of the Supreme Court in keeping the public power of nation and states within constitutional bounds.

## II. *The Record of the Court*

It is a first principle of effective federal government, as of all government, that the cloth must fit the figure, and no less so when the figure expands in size and changes its dimensions. From time to time this working principle has been threatened by decisions of the Court. The *Dred Scott* case[15] was perhaps the most dramatic, though it is doubtful whether the gathering tensions in the nation could have been dispelled by a decision recognizing power in the national government to deal with slavery in the territories. Following the Civil War the Reconstruction Acts were dampened in the *Civil Rights Cases*,[16] which reflected the sentiment that reunion called for a mitigation of the upheaval produced by the Reconstruction legislation. But even within the confines of the Fourteenth Amendment as there interpreted—as applicable to state action and not to that of public utilities—considerable scope was left for Congress to promote universal standards of civil rights under the Amendment's enabling clause.[17] Whatever uncertainty there may have been in the cases on segregation in the schools, it is scarcely to be doubted that if Congress itself had pronounced the doom of segregated primary education in the public schools the mandate would have been cheerfully accepted by the Supreme Court. And in the white primary cases, the company town cases, and the restrictive covenant cases, the Court has shown that the concept of private action must yield to a conception of state action where public functions are being performed or a state agency is the dominant source of discrimination.[18] If Congress were to address itself to a revision of the archaic and patchwork civil rights legislation it would find, within the limits set by the Court, substantial latitude for extending the standards of uniformity governing the area of civil rights.

In the field of economic regulation there have been impediments, serious but not insuperable. It is noteworthy that only in the case of the income tax was it found necessary to overcome by constitutional amendment a Supreme Court decision in the economic field.[19] Of the several constitutional amendments that have been submitted by Congress to the states and not ratified, only the child labor proposal reflected an effort to surmount a Supreme Court decision.[20] The early decisions under the Sherman Act, holding woodenly that manufacture is not commerce, were short-lived.[21] And although the conception of national economic power had not crystallized by the time of the New Deal, there were decisions, particularly those involving the regulation of transportation and restraints of trade, that would have sufficed in the hands of a Marshall to validate the major measures taken in the depression. The Court indicated its different temper clearly enough when antitrust precedents that had been applied to labor activities were held inapplicable to sustain federal regulation of trade practices and labor conditions in the same industries under the NRA and the Bituminous Coal Act, and when the transportation precedents were denied application to the Railroad Retirement Act.[22] Government by the judges, in the sense intended by critics of judicial review here and abroad, was upon us. It would appear that, like Margaret Fuller, the Court then decided to accept the Universe. Our system of judicial review produces frustrations but has a saving quality of resiliency.

In a successful Federalism opportunities must be seized for a wide variety of experiments in co-operation. The conventional picture of a modern federal system with apoplexy at the center and anemia at the extremities is not an inevitable one if various kinds of circulatory pumps are utilized. The Court has been particularly successful in finding vindication for these experiments and indeed in stimulating them. "Undoubtedly," Chief Justice Fuller observed in *Leisy v. Hardin*, "there is difficulty in drawing the line between the municipal powers of the one government and the commercial powers of the other, but when that line is determined, in the particular instance, accommodation to it, without serious inconvenience, may readily be found, to use the language of Mr. Justice Johnson, in *Gibbons v. Ogden* . . . in 'a frank and candid co-operation for the general good.' "[23] The co-operation thus invited has taken many forms and has been hospitably received. The device of the Webb-Kenyon Act,[24] "divesting" articles of their interstate character upon reaching a state, is the most familiar. The constitutional doubts about it were serious enough to induce President Taft to veto that Act, and it was preserved as a model only by virtue of the overriding of the veto.[25]

Co-operation has taken other forms. The device of a conditional grant by Congress to the states has furnished the basis for a federal-state unemployment insurance program, providing a measure of uniformity of standards but with local administration and enough diversity to embrace both the Wisconsin plant-reserve system and the more common state-wide pooled insurance fund.[26] In judicial administration, too, working methods of co-operation have been devised and successfully executed. The diversity of citizenship jurisdiction of the federal courts is a familiar instance, under which a cause of action resting on state law is adjudicated in a federal tribunal according to federal procedure. Conversely, Congress may require the state courts to entertain causes of action under federal law, as for example under the Federal Employers Liability Act and the Price Control Act, at least where there are state tribunals competent to adjudicate comparable cases under their own law.[27] Again, compacts between the states with the consent of Congress have received a full measure of encouragement from the Court, even where some adroit skirting of state constitutional obstacles has been required.[28]

When all of this has been said, it remains true that the role of the Court in these matters has been simply to place its imprimatur upon measures and devices worked out by the legislatures. If judicial review in a federal system were to be appraised solely on the basis of control over national legislation or co-operative measures, the cost in terms of doubt and occasional delay might outweigh the value. But judicial review is intended pre-eminently as a restraint on state action, and it is to that field that we must turn for a proper evaluation of the role of the Court—perhaps most vividly performed in its judgments on state measures affecting interstate commerce.

Here the Court has been more successful in its specific practical judgments than in the formulation of governing standards. The Court has worked with standards too frequently mechanical and formalistic. Where does national power end and state power begin in the control over goods shipped from one state to another? When Marshall invoked the original-package formula —the doctrine that the power of a state over imports does not attach until the original package is broken or the goods have been resold locally—he was perhaps drawing, in typical lawyer's fashion, on a concept from another branch of juristic learning, the criminal law, where the doctrine of "breaking bulk" had been devised to extend the crime of larceny to the case of a servant who, having been entrusted with goods, converted them to his own use.[29] At all events, the original-package doctrine in constitutional law soon reflected the inadequacies of reliance on a mechanical formula to resolve claims of power. A state, it is now clear, may exclude diseased or falsely labeled products in whatever package, and on the other hand it may not prohibit the resale of goods, even after the original package is broken, if its permission to sell is conditioned on a minimum price paid by the seller to an out-of-state producer.[30] No more workable have been the formalistic tests essaying a distinction between laws regulating commerce and those regulating health or safety. A state law limiting the speed at which an interstate train may travel is, to the pragmatic eye, a regulation neither exclusively of commerce nor exclusively of safety but is rather something of both, and we do not escape a hard question of judgment by converting the problem of accommodation into one of semantics.

Another standard the Court has employed to test the regulatory power of the states is the rule that a state law may not discriminate against interstate commerce. But discrimination does not wear its badge upon its sleeve, and certain forms of legislation may, depending on the point of view, be regarded as discrimination or simply as equalization. Consider, for example, the case involving the ordinance of Madison, Wisconsin, which prohibited the sale of milk as pasteurized unless it was processed and bottled at an approved plant within five miles of the center of the city.[31] To Justices Black, Douglas, and Minton the measure was a legitimate one for the control of sanitary standards, applicable alike to local and out-of-state dealers. To a majority of the

Court, however, the ordinance was an illegitimate promotion of a local monopoly of the business of pasteurization. The majority pointed out that the city might maintain its sanitary standards for milk by excluding milk not pasteurized in accordance with the standards enforced by the city, without requiring that the process be carried out at a local plant. This suggestion is a happy illustration of the technique of adjusting the claims of local welfare to those of the national market by insisting that restrictive measures in the state of destination interfere no more with interstate commerce than is consistent with the satisfaction of a genuine local need. But the suggestion raises the more general question whether equalization enforced by a state—in requiring that interstate operations measure up to local standards—is consistent with the constitutional demands of a national market.

It would be easy to answer the problem of state-imposed equalization by setting up one or another polar formula, as, for example, that equality is not discrimination or that enforced equality is a form of flexible tariff that it is the purpose of the commerce clause to forestall. In fact, the Court has slipped between the horns of the dilemma. States may not exclude out-of-state goods manufactured under conditions of child labor or other substandard working conditions; indeed it was this inability, coupled with the Court's decision striking down the Federal Child Labor Act, that created a no man's land in the federal system until the *Child Labor* case was overruled.[32] Nor may a state, to protect its local system of minimum prices for producers, prohibit goods from being brought in and sold if they were purchased outside at less than the prices set by law within.[33] But a rather different approach has been taken to the problem of taxation. The sales tax, which it was assumed could not be imposed by the state of destination in respect of goods ordered from without, placed purely local sales at a competitive disadvantage if the state of origin has no sales tax or was likewise powerless to impose one on interstate transactions. The competitive gap was closed through the introduction of a compensating use tax in the state of destination; by this device purchasers are taxed (the sellers being made liable for collection) but a credit is allowed for any sales tax paid on the same transaction. Thus the purchaser from a local seller pays only the sales tax; the purchaser from an out-of-state seller pays the corresponding use tax; and the tax burden on the competing transactions is equalized. This device has passed muster in the Court.[34] But it would be extremely unsafe to regard this judgment as a germinal decision forecasting approval for other forms of state equalization of interstate and local tax burdens.

The Court has power to allow or disallow state taxes but not to alter or set terms, and the mesh of its net is consequently coarse. The question is whether it is coarser than it needs to be. Is there any justification for the rule of thumb that the obligation of a business engaged in both intrastate and interstate commerce to pay a license tax depends on whether the taxing statute imposes the exaction on account of the intrastate commerce or indifferently on account of both?[35] Is the rule formalistic only, without rational basis in the protection of interstate commerce? Two possible grounds of support have been advanced. It is said, first, that the enterprise must be free to give up its intrastate business and escape the tax on the rest, and if it is thus free, the tax is validly imposed. But where the enterprise, though legally free to withdraw from intrastate business, could not do so in practice because that intrastate business is necessary to the profitability of the whole, the test appears a barren one.[36] Secondly, it is argued that a license tax "on" interstate as well as intrastate activities would subject the enterprise to the threat of expulsion from interstate business for failure to pay the tax. But this ground would be more persuasive if and when the state resorted to exclusionary sanctions rather than the normal modes of tax collection.[37] The real danger lurking in the formal subject of a tax is something different: the selectivity of the tax may conceal a discrimination against those economic functions that are interstate, and its burden may more readily be shifted to those outside the state. In this view the Court has understandably looked askance at selective license fees of fixed amount, varying widely among classes of enterprise—as, for example, the license fees on "drummers." [38] But the Court has not always focused squarely on this element of possible discrimination and perhaps cannot be expected to, given an admittedly wide area of permissible classification in a state's taxing system.

If we turn from the formal subjects of taxation to the measure of the tax, federalism presents still greater complexities. Seizing both horns of the dilemma, one horn playing the melody that interstate commerce must be free of taxation and the other that even interstate commerce must pay its way, the Court has scarcely resolved the dissonance. But a purer tone would give a poorer tune. If the states may tax interstate commerce but not too much, the Court's role is to decide how much is too much. Here enters the concept of allocation. Like the ideas of discrimination and equalization, it is a most suggestive criterion, which calls for some care in application.

At least three levels of problems are encountered in judging allocation formulas. First, the formula should be germane to the subject or base of the tax; the measure should be relevant to what is being measured. A property tax on mobile railroad cars calls for an allocation formula designed to yield the average daily presence of cars within the state, as if the tax were imposed on tax day once a year.[39] But even the concept of presence can prove to be a stumbling block, as in the case of aircraft. Shall these be taxed on the basis of an allocation of the total fleet which takes account of miles flown over the state or only on the number of planes arriving and departing, and if a compound formula is used, how shall the ratios be weighted in the allocation formula?[40] How shall net income from interstate business be apportioned? How much weight should be attributed to the presence of manufacturing facilities and how much to the presence of customers who have bought the product? The Court has been quite tolerant of allocation formulas save where they confer a strikingly inappropriate share of the total on a given state.[41] Perhaps tolerance has proceeded too far at times, particularly where the erratic operation of the formula has been excused by invoking as the subject matter of the tax the convenient vagueness of a franchise to do business.[42] These problems of allocation, it will be observed, would exist even if each state were to adopt the same formula. In constitutional terms, they present problems of territorial reach under the due process clause.

But in most instances, for want of a uniform act or an interstate compact, it is artificial to assume that each state will adopt the same formula, and so a second layer of problems is reached—the pyramiding of local taxes by reason of different allocation formulas in various states. To the extent that the several formulas adopted in different states are intrinsically reasonable, more than one hundred per cent of the income or property of an interstate enterprise may be taken in the aggregate as a tax base. The commerce clause thus reinforces the due process clause and may be thought to call for enforced selection of a single formula for a given class of taxes. This step the Court has been unwilling to take, as it has been unwilling for most purposes to utilize the full faith and credit clause in order to impose a single choice-of-law rule on the states in questions of conflict of laws.[43] If it is implicit in the commerce clause that an interstate business shall not be subjected to multistate fiscal charges greater in the aggregate than would have been imposed had the same volume of business been carried on within one state, the Court may be thought to be remiss in its duty toward the protection of interstate commerce.

Manifestly, however, such an ideal is incapable of achievement by the judicial process. This realization brings us to the third level of complexity. Not only is it impracticable to compare the burdens under different forms of taxation in the varying tax patterns of the several states, ranging from extraction taxes through property taxes to payroll and other excises, but even a common allocation formula for a particular tax gives no assurance of a nicely limited aggregate burden. For the allocation controls only one factor in the tax; the rates and valuations may differ from state to state and thus produce a total tax quite different from that which would have been imposed on the total enterprise had it been conducted wholly within any one state. No court can be expected to set the rates and assessment levels for a state, so long as there is no improper discrimination within the state.

The impulse at this point is to suggest the establishment by Congress of an administrative commission that would take over the function of resolving these contests over the taxation of interstate business. Such a commission would function under both the commerce clause and the enabling clause of the Fourteenth Amendment. It must be acknowledged that a commission would enjoy the strategic advantage of having power to prescribe rules and formulas, instead of merely issuing assents or vetoes. The commission would presumably acquire *expertise* in measuring the economic consequences of various forms of taxation. By taking continuous thought it could elaborate more comprehensively than the Court has done a philosophy of protection for interstate commerce. It could tell us what it means for interstate commerce to pay its way and whether interstate commerce is paying more or less than its way under a variety of fiscal burdens.

Attractive as is the case for an administrative commission, we face the basic query whether we are prepared to pay the price for this greater certainty and clarity. If a commission were to move substantially beyond the point of the Court's control of taxation, it would have to cut deep into the taxing systems of the state, determining tax rates and valuations for interstate business much as the Interstate Commerce Commission does in the more limited area of railroad charges. In any event, when we enter so sensitive and vital an area as taxation, we may be unprepared to accept the edict of a body neither so detached from the pressures of the interested parties as the Supreme Court nor so frankly responsive as the Congress. Perhaps here, as in our party system and elsewhere, a little fuzziness and untidiness at the edges, a little ground for maneuver within the confines of federalism, is an indispensable price for loyalty to the system. The problem of judicial review merges here into the larger problems of popular government and custom.

## III. *Conditions for the Success of Judicial Review*

The first requisite for one who sits in judgment on legislative acts is that he be a philosopher. He must be able to see social and economic measures under the aspect, if not of eternity, at least of a wide perspective. When critics of judicial review speak of government by judges they refer in the main to review under such vague rubrics as due process of law and equal protection of the law; but review of the federal balance is not essentially of a different order. The limitations of minds conditioned to a familiar pattern of government intervention are exposed no less in judging issues of federal-state power than in weighing claims of individuals against government. Indeed, it would be the grossest fiction to ignore the fact that the issues of federalism are contests between persons in private character and others in official character, whatever the legal framework of the controversy. In this respect our judicial process, which frequently leaves the claims of state or federal power to be asserted by private persons in opposition to duties imposed by the other sovereign, and which may thus seem to favor an artificial mode of presentation, is actually showing a high degree of realism.

When our judges refused to apply the precedents of the antitrust laws to other federal controls imposed on the same industries but reflecting a different economic philosophy—when, that is, the NRA and the Bituminous Coal Act were held to be beyond federal power—the judges were imprisoned by the same formulas that had become notorious in review under the due process clauses. The phenomenon is not peculiarly American. In Canada and Australia, where "government by judges" does not include judicial vetoes under a due process clause, the same confusion of the familiar with the permissible has confounded the umpiring of the federal system.[44]

The years 1935 to 1937 were years of decision in Canada and Australia as well as in the United States. The Canadian New Deal program of the Bennett administration came before the Privy Council in a group of cases in 1937. In order to appreciate the results, it should be remembered that under the British North America Act (1867) the Dominion has power "to make Laws for the Peace, Order, and good Government of *Canada*, in relation to all Matters not coming within the Classes of Subjects by this Act assigned exclusively to the Legislatures of the Provinces." For "greater Certainty, but not so as to restrict the Generality of the foregoing,"[45] exclusive legislative authority was conferred on the Dominion Parliament over some twenty-nine classes of subjects, including trade and commerce, bankruptcy, the criminal law, and banking; each province, at the same time, was authorized to legislate in relation to such matters as incorporation of companies with provincial objects, direct taxation within the province, and property and civil rights in the province. Over the subject of agriculture (as well as immigration) Dominion and provinces were given concurrent jurisdiction, the Dominion to prevail in case of conflict. Despite these sweeping grants of power to the Dominion, motivated in 1867 by the example of the weakness of the American Union, the Privy Council struck down Dominion statutes providing for unemployment insurance, minimum wages and maximum hours of labor, and marketing quotas for agricultural products.[46] But the entire New Deal program was not destroyed: statutes authorizing creditor's compositions for farmers were sustained, as were prohibitions on secret rebates and price discriminations engaged in to eliminate competition.[47] The pattern of decisions is less explicable in terms of a constitutional division of powers than in terms of a conception that the function of government is to maintain a free field with no favor and not to rationalize or supersede managerial planning.

The Australian experience has been similar. Rejecting the double listing of the Canadian constitution, the Australian constitution of 1900 resembles ours in its plan of enumeration of national powers, including legislative authority over trade and commerce. Section 92 declares: "On the imposition of uniform duties of customs, trade, commerce, and intercourse among the States, whether by means of internal carriage or ocean navigation, shall be absolutely free." This mandate, with its somewhat rhetorical flourish at the end, was designed to end customs barriers between the states—what had come to be termed the barbarism of borderism. In the hands of the judges, however, it has become a banner of free enterprise. Not only state legislation imposing marketing quotas on agricultural products, but national legislation of the same kind, has been overturned.[48] Indeed, the Bank Nationalization Act, under which private banking would have been taken over entirely by the Commonwealth, was wrecked on the reef of Section 92, in spite of the constitutional powers of the federal government to legislate with respect to banking and to acquire property for public use.[49]

All of this suggests that in the selection of judges for a supreme tribunal in a federation, much more is to be looked for than conventional professional attainments. It is hardly the supreme qualification for a constitutional judge that he be expert in the drawing and interpretation of wills, or even that he be experienced in the ordinary judicial business of courts having little or no responsibility in the decision of constitutional questions. As Professor Chafee remarked concerning the opposition to the appointment of Mr. Hughes as chief justice, it is less revealing to examine the list of clients in the nominee's office than to investigate the books in his library.[50]

If the first requisite of a constitutional judge is that he be a philosopher, the second requisite is that he be not too philosophical. Success in the undertaking requires absorption in the facts rather than deduction from large and rigidly held abstractions. The constitutional judge is an architect, one who tempers the vision of the artist with a reliable knowledge of the strengths and weaknesses and availability of materials. Some of the least satisfactory constitutional decisions, as the experience in Canada particularly illustrates, have taken the form of advisory opinions rendered without benefit of a detailed factual record.[51] In the familiar phrase, judgment from speculation should yield to judgment from experience.

These reflections have a bearing on the organization and procedures of a judiciary in a federal system. Review by the supreme tribunal ought not be precipitate. Ordinarily it should await the development of a body of evidence illuminating the actual working of the laws in question. There should, at the same time, be sufficient flexibility in procedure to expedite cases where exceptionally prompt decisions would be more desirable than a fuller development of the facts. A certain amount of discretion with regard to expedition or temporizing ought to be left to the court, at the risk of criticism that the court is avoiding unpleasant duties. Is not this the lesson to be drawn from the recent experience in Germany, when the court at Karlsruhe avoided a decision on the validity of the European defense treaties in advance of the vote on ratification and the national elections? The court was thus able to avoid entanglement in the political process, to remind the executive and legislative branches in effect that their responsibility could not properly be shifted to the court, and withal to preserve the prestige of an institution that must secure its position for inescapable tasks in the future.

In suggesting that the judges must be philosophers and yet not too philosophical, I am side-stepping the question, fascinating in academic circles, whether pragmatism is a philosophy or an excuse for not having a philosophy. However that may be, one can find in the thought of John Dewey a highly relevant warning against the needlessly divisive influence of abstract philosophic premises, and an appeal to the process of accommodation and adjustment for the business of living which is exemplified in the adjudicating function of a constitutional judge.

> What we want light upon is this or that group of individuals, this or that concrete human being, this or that special institution or social arrangement. For such a logic of inquiry, the traditionally accepted logic substitutes discussion of the meaning of concepts and their dialectical relationship to one another. The discussion goes on in terms of *the* state, *the* individual; the nature of institutions as such, society in general.
>
> We need guidance in dealing with particular perplexities in domestic life, and are met by dissertations on the Family or by assertions of the sacredness of individual Personality. We want to know about the

worth of the institution of private property as it operates under given conditions of definite time and place. We meet with the reply of Proudhon that property generally is theft, or with that of Hegel that the realization of will is the end of all institutions, and that private ownership as the expression of mastery of personality over physical nature is a necessary element in such realization. Both answers may have a certain suggestiveness in connection with specific situations. But the conceptions are not proffered for what they may be worth in connection with special historic phenomena. They are general answers supposed to have a universal meaning that covers and dominates all particulars. Hence they do not assist inquiry. They close it. They are not instrumentalities to be employed and tested in clarifying concrete social difficulties. They are ready-made principles to be imposed upon particulars in order to determine their nature. . . .

The waste of mental energy due to conducting discussion of social affairs in terms of conceptual generalities is astonishing. How far would the biologist and the physician progress if when the subject of respiration is under consideration, discussion confined itself to bandying back and forth the concepts of organ and organism? . . . Not only does the solemn reiteration of categories of individual and organic or social whole not further these definite and detailed inquiries, but it checks them. It detains thought within pompous and sonorous generalities wherein controversy is as inevitable as it is incapable of solution. It is true enough that if cells were not in vital interaction with one another, they could neither conflict nor cooperate. But the fact of the existence of an "organic" social group, instead of answering any questions merely marks the fact that questions exist: Just what conflicts and what cooperations occur, and what are their specific causes and consequences? [52]

This philosophy (or lack of philosophy) has come to be regarded as peculiarly American. In speaking of university studies in the social sciences in prewar Germany, Franz Neumann has pictured the transition from that environment to America:

> The whole theoretical-historical approach is (or rather was) accompanied by contempt for Anglo-American philosophy. I still hear the sneers of my philosophy professor about Locke, Condillac, and Dewey, while Whitehead was treated with silence then as now.
>
> Thus, on the whole, the German exile, bred in the veneration of theory and history, and contempt for empiricism and pragmatism, entered a diametrically opposed intellectual climate: optimistic, empirically oriented, a-historical, but also self-righteous.[53]

The question is thus raised whether the pragmatic institution of judicial review is possible in a federal system only where deep philosophic cleavages do not exist—whether judicial review is in fact a luxury reserved for those communities that can afford to focus attention on methods and arrangements rather than on basic conceptions of freedom or property or the state. It has indeed been suggested that judicial review in America is a corollary of our philosophic poverty. Louis Hartz has written:

> Looked at from a slightly different angle, however, it is this unanimity around the Lockean idea which makes the institution of judicial review, apart again from the matter of federalism, a meaningful thing. When half of a nation believes in Locke and half in Filmer or Marx, the result is not law but philosophy. *Inter arma leges silent.* But when the whole of a nation agrees on Locke, the idea of settling ultimate issues of public policy through adjudication logically arises, since the problem is then not one of principle, but of application. America's famous legalism is thus the reverse side of its philosophic poverty in politics, both of which, like its pragmatism, trace back in large part to a deep and implicit liberal general will.[54]

Although Professor Hartz excludes from his analysis judicial review in matters of federalism, the exclusion may be an unnecessary concession, inasmuch as the process can involve issues as deep-cutting as those subsumed under other constitutional provisions. Thus the question of segregation in the public schools is an issue of federalism, stemming from the post-Civil-War mandate that in matters of civil rights we are to be one people governed by national and not state standards. And so, with federalism presently an object of world fascination, the question raised by Professor Hartz must be faced if we are to consider whether our experience has relevance for other peoples—whether the institution of judicial review in a federal system is an exportable product.

The philosophic unity that can be pointed to in America serves to conceal conflicts over programs of action which may be as intense as those to be found in countries where controversy over philosophic premises is more rampant. We may all be said to accept the institution of property in America, and yet this attachment to a common concept did not forestall the tension of the sit-down strikes in the depression of the nineteen-thirties, nor was the tension dissipated because the workers appealed to the notion of a property right in their jobs and the employers to a property right in the premises. While we may all profess allegiance to the constitutional principle of the free exercise of religion, the practical issue of state aid to religious schools is not thereby averted; under the common standard are ranged those who insist that religion presupposes a religious element in education, as well as those who maintain that religion is best served through divorcement from secular education. The pragmatist is obstinate enough to insist that the most meaningful unities and disunities are to be found in the realm of programs of action rather than in philosophic slogans.

If this is so, the judicial process as it has evolved in this country is not without meaning for other communities.

That meaning may be found, not in the arrogant assumption that principles may be dispensed with, but in the introduction of mediating principles between the large constitutional or philosophical concepts to which some or all of a community pay tribute and the common problems of reconciliation which beset the modern state. In the same symposium at which Professor Neumann spoke of the social sciences, the theologian Paul Tillich described the way in which Europe and America made their distinctive contributions in the realm of theology:

> The difficulties, stressed by Continental theology, in applying the absolute principles of the Christian message to concrete political situations, were met by American theological ethics in a rather ingenious way. One found that between the absolute principle of love and the ever-changing concrete situation, middle axioms exist which mediate the two. Such principles are democracy, the dignity of every man, equality before the law, etc. They are not unchangeable in the sense in which the ultimate principle is, but they mediate between it and the actual situation. This idea prevents the identification of the Christian message with a special political program. It makes it, on the other hand, possible for Christianity not to remain aloof from the actual problems of man's historical existence.[55]

The role of the courts in maintaining a working federalism is precisely this task of mediation between large principles and particular problems, the task of interposing intermediate principles more tentative, experimental, and pragmatic. The courts are the substations that transform the high-tension charge of the philosophers into the reduced voltage of a serviceable current. At the risk of making oneself an exhibit of Professor Neumann's self-righteous scholar and a caricature of Professor Hartz's American constitutional lawyer, one may suggest that judicial review in a federal system is an exercise in the kind of thinking most needed in the modern state. For judicial review is not merely a derivative from a society in agreement on fundamentals; in itself it is an educative and formative influence that, like the legal idea of a fair trial, may have consequences beyond its immediate application for the mind of a people.[56] It would be a happy augury if a people were to become better empiricists in the process of becoming more effective federalists.

# V. PORTRAIT OF A LIBERAL JUDGE: MR. JUSTICE BRANDEIS

The appointment of a lawyer to the Supreme Court tempts us to inquire into his earlier career, and particularly the economic interests he represented, for a clue to his future performance as a judge. What is past is prologue, to be sure; but the drama as it unfolds may be full of surprise. A crude economic interpretation of the judicial office ignores too many elements of character. The taking of the robe, an experience at once emancipating and humbling, is apt to dissolve old ties and to quicken the sense that there is no escape from that judgment of one's successors which is called history.

The record of the Court is full of cautions against the generalization that the lawyer is father to the judge. It was a successful lawyer for shipping interests, Henry Billings Brown, who, as Mr. Justice Brown, delivered a memorable dissent in the cases that invalidated the income tax: ". . . the decision involves nothing less than a surrender of the taxing power to the moneyed class. . . . I hope it may not prove the first step toward the submergence of the liberties of the people in a sordid despotism of wealth." [1] It was a successful railroad lawyer, Stanley Matthews, once rejected by the Senate because of his clientele, who, as Mr. Justice Matthews, expressed what is perhaps the most salient proposition of constitutional law next to Marshall's "We must never forget, that it is a constitution we are expounding." Mr. Justice Matthews, in resisting a request that an act of Congress be declared unconstitutional, declared that the Court:

> . . . has no jurisdiction to pronounce any statute, either of a State or of the United States, void, because irreconcilable with the Constitution, except as it is called upon to adjudge the legal rights of litigants in actual controversies. In the exercise of that jurisdiction, it is bound by two rules, to which it has rigidly adhered, one, never to anticipate a question of constitutional law in advance of the necessity of deciding it; the other never to formulate a rule of constitutional law broader than is required by the precise facts to which it is to be applied. These rules are safe guides to sound judgment. It is the dictate of wisdom to follow them closely and carefully.[2]

It was another railroad lawyer, Joseph P. Bradley, who, as Mr. Justice Bradley, protested against the use of the due process clause to review the regulation of railroad rates by the states, and who would have permitted the states to regulate interstate rates until Congress assumed the responsibility.[3] And it was Harlan F. Stone, whose record in sustaining the validity of social legislation needs no comment, who had written in 1916 by way of commentary on Herbert Spencer's "The Sins of Legislators" that "Spencer's vigorous warning furnishes food for thought and will perhaps inspire with caution the zealous advocates of such sweeping legislative changes as are involved in the many proposals for the various types of pension law, and minimum wage statutes, and modern legislation of similar character." [4] The list could be extended. It is worth recalling Professor Chafee's remark, quoted in the preceding chapter, that if you want to forecast the outlook of a lawyer in judicial office, it is more important to look at the books in his library than at a list of his clients.

The instances I have given exemplify the successful caretaker of powerful groups becoming the disinterested judge. What of the lawyer who has been identified with quite different professional interests—representation of the consumer or the poorly organized, or service in the cause of law reform? For him as a judge what are the hallmarks of liberalism? Shall his judgeship be a continuance or indeed an intensification of his earlier concerns; or for him too is there a problem of adjustment to his new role, a change of pace or of direction?

I know of no better approach to this question than through the experience of Mr. Justice Brandeis. A coldly passionate and relentless adversary, he had and he showed little of the conventional respect for the captains and the kings and the mandarins in our society, while he had a fervid regard for the potentialities of the obscure. Such a man, so irreverent toward the god of things as they are, would be a clear and present danger on the bench; so at least it was thought by many.

They overlooked a number of significant factors in his social thought as a citizen and counselor at law. For one thing he was a devoted friend of private capitalism, so long as he could define what was the essence of capitalism and what its excrescences. In addition, his enormous driving force was controlled by an equally remarkable sense of balance. If he was a devil on wheels to his opponents, he was the austere judge to his clients. The role of "counsel for the situation" appealed to his constructive talents and to his faith in the power of reasoned thought to find accommodations within the framework of principle. After guiding an association of employers to victory against a striking union, he converted the congratulatory meeting into a forum for a lecture to his clients on the just claims of labor, which included a greater share in the responsibilities of industrial management. In similar vein, when addressing a gathering of labor leaders he was quick to seize the occasion as an opportunity to win their support for the unpopular cause of scientific management.[5]

But when every allowance is made for these tempering attributes, it is true that for Brandeis no less than for other judges the transition from private citizen to Supreme Court judge posed some basic issues. Many of his most deep-seated convictions were at odds not only with prevailing judicial conceptions but with the assumptions of legislators who could fairly be called progressive. What was there in the career of Brandeis as a Justice that marked him as a liberal?

He had a deeply moral, at times a moralistic, nature that unfailingly impressed itself on those who came to know him. It would have been easy to translate this quality flatly into judicial opinions, particularly into dissents when he was speaking for himself alone. But he was writing judicial opinions, not homilies. His moral nature was commanded by a disciplined morality of mind. The ethical power of his opinions is the stronger because the ethical claims of the litigants were resolved, not at large, but through the special focus of his station. His morality of mind was the essence of his liberalism as a judge, and gave a coherence to his labors that transcends his contribution to this or that particular sector of the law, impressive as those contributions have been.

I would suggest four principal manifestations of the essential quality of mind he brought to his task: (1) an insistence on knowledge as indispensable to judging; (2) rejection of opportunism; (3) an insistence on jurisdictional and procedural observances; and (4) rejection of sentimentality.

(1) In his own phrase, knowledge must precede understanding and understanding should precede judging.[6] If any *vade mecum* was inscribed on the tablets of his mind, I surmise that it would have been these words. They explain a good deal about his methods that might otherwise appear singular and unrelated. His belief in the primacy of facts was apparent even in the process of preparing an opinion. However much he encouraged his law clerks to present the results of their legal research in a form that might be directly useful in drafting an opinion, he took on himself the burden of drafting the statement of facts. This was his private assurance that he would not be seduced by the fascination of legal analysis until he had grounded himself in the realities of the case as they were captured in the record.

It was essentially the same sense of the controlling vitality of facts that produced the so-called Brandeis brief at the bar and its counterpart in his richly documented opinions on the bench. No one attached more weight than he to the presumption of constitutionality attaching to acts of the legislature; and yet he was rarely content to rest his judgment there without the confirmation that he found in a study of the context of legislation. In his opinions the technique of the Brandeis brief was generally employed to sustain the legislative judgment. But on occasion the same technique, reflecting the same insatiable passion to know, was employed to suggest that what had once been constitutional might be questionable in the light of facts that had markedly changed. A remand of the cause for further findings was for him an important and valuable procedural mechanism. He employed it, for example, when he raised the question whether to place the cost of grade-crossing removal on a railroad might have become constitutionally less tolerable with the great increase in competitive traffic on the highways.[7]

This readiness to see significance in a fuller exhibit of facts, whatever the direction in which the facts might point, suggests the next aspect of the morality of his mind, namely his rejection of opportunism.

(2) It is hardly likely that anyone came to the Supreme Court with a more closely articulated set of convictions than those that Brandeis held. His views on the most specific and particular issues could be readily predicted by one who was familiar with the basic premises of his thinking. Inexorable as were the implications of these premises, they were not congenial, as I have said, to much that passed current in the world of social thought. He believed that capitalism succeeded only as it provided larger and larger opportunities for the sharing of responsibility, and that it was corrupted as power became more and more divorced from those who were its subjects. As economic controls have become more anonymous and remote, it is a commonplace that the state has felt obliged to intervene in order to mitigate the cruelties that are the residual deposit of the machine. Brandeis took a fundamentally different approach to the role of the state, conceiving it to be primarily an instrument whereby incentives are provided for the responsible and socially useful exercise of power. Hence his sovereign measure was the discouragement of bigness through a graduated tax on gross assets. Hence, too, in his conception of social security, he had a strong preference for the Wisconsin or company-reserve plan of unemployment insurance over the state-wide pooled fund; for the Wisconsin plan was meant as an incentive to each employer to regularize his employment, while the competing system was designed as a palliative for what was accepted as the inevitable and impersonal doom of unemployment under conditions of capitalism. It is no

secret that Brandeis would have welcomed a provision in the federal social security law giving credit for contributions made only pursuant to a state plan of the Wisconsin type. But the prevailing philosophy, for better or for worse, was to the contrary, a philosophy influenced by the experience of social workers and the popular spread of insurance. Despite the disappointment, Brandeis did not hesitate to join in upholding the pooled-reserve plan as constitutional.[8]

He had other, similar convictions, which might have appeared whimsical or crotchety had they not derived from what were to him fundamental principles of a working capitalism. Consider, for example, so seemingly trivial a matter as fidelity insurance. He considered it, in a word, as an abomination—and the word is his—for to him it was the very negation of managerial responsibility to divest itself of the duty and risk of knowing the character of trusted employees.[9] Yet I daresay no one will be heard to suggest that in his judgments on the bench fidelity insurance fared badly on that account.

The principle of informed vigilance as the soul of business enterprise was likewise violated in his view by the practice of large depositors, particularly public bodies, taking a pledge of assets from a bank to secure their deposits. Not only was the practice prejudicial to the ordinary unsecured depositor—Brandeis liked to point out that the familiar banking sign "Government Depositary" was apt to be quite misleading to the small customer—but in addition it removed an incentive for vigilance on the part of government authorities in supervising banks in which government deposits were placed. He believed, for example, that a spectacular bank failure in New York might have been averted had the state retained this incentive. On the bench he did indeed write an opinion for the Court holding that national banks lacked power to secure the deposits of private customers by pledging assets; but he joined with the Court in interpreting an amendment to the National Banking Act as validating retroactively the pledging of assets to secure the deposits of states and their subdivisions.[10]

In constitutional law as well he was obliged on occasion to subordinate his deeply held convictions to the canons of his office. During the depression he kept a file, labeled with characteristic directness "Depression Cures." I am certain that far down on the list in his own evaluation came schemes for the limiting of production. And yet none of his opinions showed more laborious or earnest effort than his dissent in the *New State Ice* case, arguing for the authority of Oklahoma to limit access to the ice business by the issuance of certificates of convenience and necessity. Only a note of skepticism, uncommon in his opinions, served to betray his private judgment of the law:

> The objections to the proposal are obvious and grave. The remedy might bring evils worse than the present disease. The obstacles to success seem insuperable. The economic and social sciences are largely uncharted seas. We have been none too successful in the modest essays in economic control already entered upon. The new proposal involves a vast extension of the area of control. Merely to acquire the knowledge essential as a basis for the exercise of this multitude of judgments would be a formidable task; and each of the thousands of these judgments would call for some measure of prophecy. Even more serious are the obstacles to success inherent in the demands which execution of the project would make upon human intelligence and upon the character of men. Man is weak and his judgment is at best fallible.
>
> Yet the advances in the exact sciences and the achievements in invention remind us that the seemingly impossible sometimes happens. . . .
>
> To stay experimentation in things social and economic is a grave responsibility. Denial of the right to experiment may be fraught with serious conse-

quences to the Nation. It is one of the happy incidents of the federal system that a single courageous State may, if its citizens choose, serve as a laboratory; and try novel social and economic experiments without risk to the rest of the country. This Court has the power to prevent an experiment. We may strike down the statute which embodies it on the ground that, in our opinion, the measure is arbitrary, capricious or unreasonable. We have power to do this, because the due process clause has been held by the Court applicable to matters of substantive law as well as to matters of procedure. But in the exercise of this high power, we must be ever on our guard, lest we erect our prejudices into legal principles. If we would guide by the light or reason, we must let our minds be bold.[11]

At the following term he delivered another elaborate dissent, this time in support of the power of Florida to impose graduated taxes on chain stores proportionate to the number of counties in which they operated.[12] Here his legislative judgment coincided entirely with his judicial judgment, and the opinion was a labor of love; but it was no more zealous and thoroughgoing than the dissent of the term before.

In one of his most massive and deeply felt opinions, the *Myers* case,[13] Brandeis in dissent argued that the Senate could be given power to share in the removal of executive officials whose appointment it had confirmed. This position, counter to that of President Wilson, was buttressed by considerations of democratic political theory that commended themselves to Brandeis. When, later, the question arose of the power of the Senate to withdraw its confirmation of a nominee to the Federal Power Commission during the interval provided by the Senate rules but after the commission had been delivered, it might have been supposed that Brandeis would again have espoused the cause of the Senate, particularly since the Senate's reconsideration was due to what it regarded as the reactionary views of the nominee on issues of a public power policy. And yet where Brandeis had been insistent in opposing the position of his sponsor Wilson, he was the author of the Court's opinion sustaining the position of President Hoover against the Senate.[14] The legal and historical sources pointed differently, in his view, on the two problems. They were not to be resolved by the expediency of the occasion or even simply by large generalizations about the distribution of authority in a democratic state.

An experiment that Brandeis watched with the utmost sympathy was the Tennessee Valley Authority. Like co-operatives, it provided a new form of enterprise in which the energies and imagination of large numbers of people could be enlisted; and it provided something of a measuring rod for more conventional forms of enterprise. When the first test came of the constitutional basis for the sale of commercial power by the Authority, a majority of the Court, led by Chief Justice Hughes, sustained the activity. While Brandeis by no means disagreed as a matter of constitutional law, he was of opinion that the shareholders' suit by which the question was presented was not a proper vehicle to reach the constitutional question, and he therefore concurred in the result, but on procedural grounds.[15] The opportunity to obtain a basic validation of TVA was less important to him than the maintenance of proper standards of judicial review.

And so we are led to look more closely into what I have called his insistence on jurisdictional and procedural observances.

(3) It has sometimes been said that Brandeis was a liberal in social and economic thought and a conservative in matters of legal procedure. The truth is that his procedural attitudes were part and parcel of those qualities of mind which made him a liberal. He did indeed dissent alone from the promulgation of the *Federal Rules of Civil Procedure*. His reasons were not publicly stated, but they are not unknown. Partly he

was unwilling to take the responsibility for a complicated formulation to which he as well as other members of the Court had been able to give only limited consideration. Partly he was influenced by an apprehension that the rules might become as intricate as the codification of civil practice in New York, which was hardly to be preferred to the simple Massachusetts system under which he had practiced. Finally, the devotion to the federal principle which motivated his opinion in *Erie Railroad v. Tompkins*,[16] enforcing conformity to state rules of decision in the federal courts, led him likewise to reject the idea of nationalization of rules of procedure for the federal courts.

It is true also that he set himself firmly against declaratory judgments, yielding only when Congress authorized them "in cases of actual controversy." [17] One may venture to suggest that he was no more opposed to declaratory judgments for the staple business of state courts than he was to the adoption by state courts of many of the specific reforms in the *Federal Rules of Civil Procedure*. What he discerned in declaratory judgments was a device, only somewhat less objectionable than advisory opinions, that might be used to bring before the courts questions of the validity of statutes at what he regarded as a premature stage. It was too easy by these means to expose the legislative plant to the judicial blight before it had come to full fruition. The experience in some states had shown the truth of Laertes's words, "The canker galls the infants of the spring too oft before their buttons are disclosed."

What may appear in isolation to be surprisingly conservative responses to procedural reforms turn out to be phases of a pervading philosophy—the faithful maintenance of the federal balance and the fullest scope for experimentation by legislatures free of judicial constraint.

His respect for the spheres of competence of other

organs of authority showed itself in his forbearance when sitting in judgment on the decisions of administrative agencies. But they forfeited their claim when they in turn failed to observe procedural guarantees. "The mere admission by an administrative tribunal," Brandeis said, "of matter which under the rules of evidence applicable to judicial proceedings would be deemed incompetent . . . or mere error in reasoning upon evidence introduced, does not invalidate an order. But where rates found by a regulatory body to be compensatory are attacked as being confiscatory, courts may enquire into the method by which its conclusion was reached. An order based upon a finding made without evidence . . . or upon a finding made upon evidence which clearly does not support it . . . is an arbitrary act against which courts afford relief." [18]

Moreover, procedures for challenging administrative orders must also be adequate. Brandeis wrote a number of opinions developing the theme that if a utility is obliged to violate an order to test its validity, the penalties for violation must not be oppressive, else no fair opportunity for challenge would be provided. Consequently he was prepared to enjoin the enforcement of such penalties even though the rate order should ultimately be held valid. He explained it in this way: "If upon final hearing the maximum rates fixed should be found not to be confiscatory, a permanent injunction should, nevertheless, issue to restrain enforcement of penalties accrued *pendente lite*, provided that it also be found that the plaintiff had reasonable ground to contest them as being confiscatory." [19] Parenthetically, may not this technique suggest a suitable procedure to govern injunctions against threatened prosecution for exercising rights of speech? May not the threat of prosecution itself be a cloud on speech which is an illegitimate deterrent where the prohibition though ultimately found valid was at least questionable? That is, in proper cases may there not be a guaranteed interim period of freedom from restraint pending a final decision?

Brandeis himself recognized, in another context, that the subject matter regulated should color the procedure on review. He put it candidly in his great concurring opinion in the *St. Joseph Stock Yards* case, where he drew a distinction

> . . . between the right to liberty of person and other constitutional rights. . . . A citizen who claims that his liberty is being infringed is entitled, upon habeas corpus, to the opportunity of a judicial determination of the facts. And, so highly is this liberty prized, that the opportunity must be accorded to any resident of the United States who claims to be a citizen. . . . But a multitude of decisions tells us that when dealing with property a much more liberal rule applies. They show that due process of law does not always entitle an owner to have the correctness of findings of fact reviewed by a court.[20]

Late in his career, in the *Senn* case, he stated by way of dictum that "Members of a union might, without special statutory authorization by a state, make known the facts of a labor dispute, for freedom of speech is guaranteed by the Federal Constitution."[21] But he was far from asserting that the admixture of elements of speech with elements of a labor controversy puts the matter beyond the pale of regulation. For immediately following the dictum he added, "The state may, in the exercise of its police power, regulate the methods and means of publicity as well as the use of public streets." There is no reason to believe that he abandoned the considered views he had expressed twenty years earlier in his dissent in the *Duplex* case, where he would have permitted labor unions to conduct a boycott of a manufacturer and his customers, adding a caveat:

> Because I have come to the conclusion that both the common law of a State and a statute of the United

> States declare the right of industrial combatants to push their struggle to the limits of the justification of self-interest, I do not wish to be understood as attaching any constitutional or moral sanction to that right. All rights are derived from the purposes of the society in which they exist; above all rights rises duty to the community. The conditions developed in industry may be such that those engaged in it cannot continue their struggle without danger to the community. But it is not for judges to determine whether such conditions exist, nor is it their function to set the limits of permissible contest and to declare the duties which the new situation demands. This is the function of the legislature which, while limiting individual and group rights of aggression and defense, may substitute processes of justice for the more primitive method of trial by combat.[22]

His respect for the competence of legislatures and boards to govern was not limited to his abstention after they had acted. More than once he insisted that the courts refrain from intervening at all because the problem lent itself potentially to full-scale administrative treatment far better than to fragmentary judicial control. Two of his most suggestive opinions, both in dissent, struck this note. In the celebrated case of *Associated Press v. International News Service*,[23] to be discussed more fully a little later in this essay, Brandeis would have had the Court do nothing to restrain the "pirating" of the plaintiff's news bulletins by the defendant, since in granting the relief the Court was creating new rights of property without the competence to impose on the successful party suitable obligations to the public in the dissemination of news. In *Pennsylvania v. West Virginia*[24] he would not have lent the aid of the Court to the plaintiff state to restrain the enforcement of a West Virginia law limiting the out-of-state shipment of natural gas; for here, too, the Court was without adequate standards to deal constructively with the problem of equitable apportionment of the industrial resources of a state. Even the traditional instrument of a court of equity, the conditional decree, may be much less adequate than a legislative standard administered by an agency continuously responsible and informed by expert judgment.

This pervading concern with the fitness of the members of the body politic for their respective tasks, this genuinely organic conception of government, encompassed the Supreme Court itself. Consequently such technical issues as the distinction between obligatory jurisdiction on appeal as against discretionary jurisdiction on certiorari assumed for Brandeis the importance of first principles.[25] He was a firm believer in limiting the jurisdiction of the Supreme Court on every front, and he would not be seduced by the quixotic temptation to right every fancied wrong that was paraded before him. The time was always out of joint but he was not born alone to set it right. Grievances set out in petitions for certiorari were examined with great dispatch, and if petitions did not carry on their face compelling reasons for granting them, they were promptly marked for denial. Husbanding his time and energies as if the next day were to be his last, he steeled himself, like a scientist in the service of man, against the enervating distraction of the countless tragedies he was not meant to relieve. His concern for jurisdictional and procedural limits reflected, on the technical level, a basic professional and personal philosophy. "Self-limitation," he liked to quote from Goethe, "is the first mark of the master." Like Epictetus he recognized "the impropriety of being emotionally affected by what is not under one's control." [26]

And so we are led to what I have called the final aspect of his morality of mind, his rejection of sentimentality.

(4) He was, to be sure, a humanitarian, as admirers are fond of saying. But he was so in a Lincolnesque

sense, even as he bore a certain resemblance to Lincoln in countenance and bearing. His devotion to a harmonious federal union, like Lincoln's, could take precedence over his immediate emotional attachments.

Within the Constitution he found resources for a strengthened federalism which had been imperfectly tapped. Among these was the full faith and credit clause, offering a means of cementing the states without superseding their authority by national legislation. He saw an opportunity to allay friction and avoid overlapping of state powers through the fuller application of this clause, and he was not deterred by the circumstance that the result in specific cases would distress his natural sympathies. In one case he insisted that an injured workman could not recover from his employer under the law of another state if the state of employment had made its compensation act the exclusive remedy.[27] In a second case he ruled that the beneficiary suing under a life insurance policy could not take advantage of the law of her present home if the law of the state where the policy was issued and where the insured had resided gave the insurance company a defense on ground of the insured's misrepresentation.[28] In a third case he maintained that a minor child could not recover additional support from her father under the law of her present residence if a judgment for support previously rendered at her father's domicile was unmodifiable by the law of that state.[29] Each of these opinions was by no means compelled by text or precedent; indeed the first of them has subsequently been overruled, and the third provoked a dissent from Justices Stone and Cardozo. Yet Brandeis was prepared to reject the claims, almost literally, of a workman, a widow, and an orphan in pursuance of what seemed to him to be a more harmonious federalism.

No one would have been more entitled, or less inclined, to echo the words of the German historian, "I have spent sleepless nights that others might rest."

Sometimes humanitarianism requires a hard choice between man and men. Jonathan Swift could say that he hated man but loved Pope and Bolingbroke. But in a great judge, as in all who have successfully shouldered the responsibility of power, sentiments of affection yield to devotion to the larger cause. To an unsentimental judge hard cases may make good law.

To find an epitome of all these elements of mind, and to see how the ethical focus of the judge gives greater dimension to the ethical problems of litigants, one can do no better than to compare the opinions of Brandeis in two cases—*Associated Press v. International News Service*,[30] and *Olmstead v. United States*.[31]

In the first, the Associated Press was suing to enjoin the International News Service from "pirating" news reports of the A.P. and making them available to subscribers of the I.N.S. The legal question was admittedly a rather novel one, in view of the special character of the legal interest in news. Three possible points of view could have been taken. First, it might have been decided that the A.P. should go without relief, on the ground that there was no recognized "property interest" in news and, on the defendant's side, no wrong that could be categorized conventionally as a passing off of one's own product as that of another. A second possibility was to maintain that the law keeps pace with the varieties of commercial interest, that the category of property is not a closed one, and that neither does the category of "passing off" exhaust the class of business torts. In fact, this was the approach taken by a majority of the Court, in a decision which has generally been regarded as a high example of progressivism in the law.

Justice Brandeis followed neither the first nor second view. To him a larger and overriding consideration was involved, that of the public interest in the dissemination of news. He recognized the wrongful character of the defendant's conduct, but he pointed out that if a court of equity was to grant the extraordinary remedy of injunction, it could not close its eyes to the position of the plaintiff as a purveyor of a necessity of modern life and as an organization dominant in its field, enjoying the benefits of restrictive bylaws that may have prevented the defendant's subscribers from sharing the plaintiff's services on a more orderly basis. In short, Justice Brandeis rejected the progressivism of the majority and did so by interpreting in the narrowest possible way the precedents and analogies that the Court relied upon. The so-called *Ticker Tape* cases, which were perhaps most closely in point, were distinguished by Brandeis as resting on breach of a confidential relationship. In another sense, Brandeis was more progressive than his brethren, since he would have placed the news service in the class of public utilities, bearing an obligation to serve all those offering to pay a reasonable charge. Since, however, such treatment could best be left to legislation, Brandeis concluded that the most just action for the Court was to take no action save to dismiss the bill of complaint.

The resemblance between the *Associated Press* case and the *Olmstead* case is evident on the surface. The latter presented the question whether wire tapping by federal officials, in violation of state law, constituted an unreasonable search and seizure in contravention of the Fourth Amendment of the federal Constitution. The classification of wire tapping within the categories of an eighteenth-century document presented the Court with another opportunity to demonstrate the adaptability of the law to advances in science and the practical arts. Here the roles were reversed. A majority of the Court refused to assimilate wire tapping to the search and seizure of premises or persons, while Brandeis's eloquent dissent is a *locus classicus* on the theme of the dynamism of law, including constitutional law. In this case the responsibility of the Court was inescapable. The issue involved the basic processes of government as they impinge on the individual against whom the forces of the law are brought to bear. In the *Associated Press* case Brandeis had been willing, indeed insistent, that the inequities of the competitive struggle be left for resolution by the legislature, lest the Court do an ill-considered job. In the *Olmstead* case the processes of the criminal law had been applied to the individual, and no agency of government more appropriate than the Court could be expected to resolve the contest between public power and personal immunity.

Even in the *Olmstead* case Brandeis did not come easily to the ultimate constitutional problem. Prior to the oral argument in the case Brandeis and his law clerk labored for several weeks in drafting an opinion resting on the doctrine of clean hands—the principle that a court of equity will not act at the suit of a litigant who is himself culpable—thus avoiding the Fourth Amendment and placing the case squarely on the irregularity of the conduct under state law. The statutes of all the states bearing on wire tapping were duly collected and abstracted, and several drafts of an opinion went through the printer's hands. After the argument the draft opinion was thoroughly reorganized. The constitutional issue was given first place, developed with a wealth of learning from English constitutional history and from the evolution of the law toward the protection of intangible interests against subtler interferences than those with which the more primitive law was concerned. Even after the opinion was thus reorganized, owing to the emphasis at the oral argument on the constitutional issue, Brandeis did not give up hope of resolving the problem on a less heroic plane. He lifted from the revised draft the portions resting on the doctrine of clean hands, had copies made by the printer, and circulated them to his brethren with the urgent suggestion that the case be disposed of on this ground. It was only after he met with rebuff in this endeavor that he pressed the constitutional dissent.

The evolution of this dissenting opinion illustrates the judicial method of Brandeis. He drew on his own experience, on his legal learning and intensive study, on contemporary facts, and on his intuition verified by these personal and vicarious experiences and by the critical analysis of his law clerk. In the *Olmstead* dissent of 1928 an early pioneering essay by Brandeis in 1890, on "The Right to Privacy," furnished useful and relevant matter. Brandeis's early law partner, Samuel Warren, had been the victim of a social gossip sheet. Under that stimulus, they proceeded to formulate a new category of legal rights. It may be of interest to set out in sequence excerpts from that article, then from a draft opinion of February 16, 1928, and finally from the opinion as it was delivered.

The essay of 1890 contained the following passages:

> Recent inventions and business methods call attention to the next step which must be taken for the protection of the person, and for securing to the individual what Judge Cooley calls the right "to be let alone." Instantaneous photographs and newspaper enterprise have invaded the sacred precincts of private and domestic life; and numerous mechanical devices threaten to make good the prediction that "what is whispered in the closet shall be proclaimed from the house-tops." . . .
>
> These considerations lead to the conclusion that the protection afforded to thoughts, sentiments, and emotions, expressed through the medium of writing or of the arts, so far as it consists in preventing publication, is merely an instance of the enforcement of the more general right of the individual to be let alone.[32]

The memorandum of February 16, 1928, contained the following passage:

> Since those days, subtler means of invading privacy and of curtailing personal liberty have been made

> available to the Government. The advances in science—discovery and invention—have made it possible for the Government to effect disclosure in court of "what is whispered in the closet"—by means far more effective than stretching the defendant upon the rack. By means of television, radium and photography, there may some day be developed ways by which the Government could, without removing papers from secret drawers, reproduce them in court and lay before the jury the most intimate occurrences of the home. It is conceivable, also, that advances in the psychic and related sciences may afford means of exploring a man's unexpressed beliefs, thoughts and emotions. Can it be that the Constitution affords no protection against such invasion by the Government of personal liberty? As has been said of much lesser intrusions, that would "place the liberty of every man in the hands of every petty officer." It would "destroy all the comforts of society." And "no man could endure to live longer in this country."[33]

Finally, the opinion as delivered included these passages:

> Discovery and invention have made it possible for the Government, by means far more effective than stretching upon the rack, to obtain disclosure in court of what is whispered in the closet.
>
> Moreover, "in the application of a constitution, our contemplation cannot be only of what has been but of what may be." The progress of science in furnishing the Government with means of espionage is not likely to stop with wire-tapping. Ways may some day be developed by which the Government, without removing papers from secret drawers, can reproduce them in court, and by which it will be enabled to expose to a jury the most intimate occurrences of the home. Advances in the psychic and related sciences may bring means of exploring unexpressed beliefs, thoughts and emotions. "That places the liberty of every man in the hands of every petty officer" was said by James Otis of much lesser intrusions than

> these. To Lord Camden, a far slighter intrusion seemed "subversive of all the comforts of society." Can it be that the Constitution affords no protection against such invasions of individual security? . . .
>
> The makers of our Constitution undertook to secure conditions favorable to the pursuit of happiness. They recognized the significance of man's spiritual nature, of his feelings and of his intellect. They knew that only a part of the pain, pleasure and satisfactions of life are to be found in material things. They sought to protect Americans in their beliefs, their thoughts, their emotions and their sensations. They conferred, as against the Government, the right to be let alone—the most comprehensive of rights and the right most valued by civilized men.[34]

It is obvious that the opinion grew in strength and eloquence as it was hammered out and as it evolved from ideas that were a response to the unpleasantness in which Samuel Warren found himself, through the principles of unclean hands, to the ultimate philosophy of man's spiritual nature which Brandeis found embodied in our Constitution. The crescendo of feeling rises from stage to stage as Brandeis is driven to explore ever more deeply the foundations of individual security.

One distinction of the draft memorandum, it may be observed in passing, was lost in the final version. The reference to television would doubtless have been the first notice of that discovery in a judicial opinion, since the working papers of the Justice show that he was relying on a newspaper account of what was then a current experiment. Unhappily the reference was deleted in deference to the skepticism of his law clerk, who strongly doubted that the new device could be adapted to the uses of espionage.

There was, finally, in Brandeis a deep institutional sense concerning his court. It showed itself in small details. Disapproving the practice of some of his colleagues of circulating draft opinions for approval just a day or two before the week-end conference, he made a point of circulating his own drafts at the beginning of the week, even if they were completed a few days before. He took a paradoxical pleasure in receiving little critical comments from his brethren on drafts of his opinions. Once, when Justice Sutherland sent such a list and the criticisms were found to be mistaken, Brandeis's law clerk, venturing in a gloating mood to make some uncomplimentary remarks about them to his justice, was quickly cut off with the comment, "I am glad that Justice Sutherland offered these criticisms, because they show that he is doing his duty in studying the opinions as they come to him." When Brandeis appeared before a Senate committee with Chief Justice Hughes and Mr. Justice Van Devanter to testify on a bill to amend the Court's jurisdiction, and was asked to add his testimony to that of his two brethren, he simply responded, "Mr. Chairman and gentlemen, the subject has been discussed so fully by the Chief Justice and Mr. Justice Van Devanter that I think I can aid you best by saying I agree absolutely with everything they have said." [35] It is quite possible that in his last official act—retirement rather than resignation—he was motivated in his choice by the fact that two of his brethren had but recently chosen retirement and he was unwilling to make an invidious departure from their practice.

His sense of institutional solidarity was stronger than his attachment to any one of his colleagues, even to Holmes. For while he avoided any act that might impair the standing of the Court, he did not indulge in monotonous or slavish agreement with his senior associate. Their disagreements were not frequent, but they were not unimportant. In two celebrated cases Holmes was led by his guiding canons to support action by a state which Brandeis regarded as an infringement of constitutional liberty. In *Gilbert v. Minnesota*[36] Holmes concurred in sustaining a conviction under a state law for discouraging enlistment in the armed forces, while Brandeis regarded the statute as too broadly drawn and in any event not applicable in a sphere where Congress alone should have authority to take protective measures. In *Meyer v. Nebraska*[37] the Court held that a state could not forbid the teaching of modern foreign languages in private schools in the elementary grades. Brandeis concurred without opinion while Holmes dissented. These two cases raised in perplexing form the dilemma facing a judge who is faithful both to the principle of local self-government and to that of freedom of the mind. In the ultimate test, Holmes as a judge set a higher value on freedom of experimentation by the state, Brandeis on freedom of experimentation in ideas. The division in these cases ought to be a sufficient caveat that the light of liberalism does not point its shafts in only one direction.

Other significant divisions occurred. In *Casey v. United States*[38] Holmes wrote for the Court sustaining the conviction of a defendant under the Narcotics Act, despite evidence in the record that the offense was committed as the result of enticement by persons under the direction of the government. Brandeis regarded the evidence as so challenging that the Court of its own motion should have directed an acquittal even though the defense of entrapment was not relied on by counsel in the case. Procedural abuses in law enforcement were for him matters that involved the integrity of the Court itself. In *Hughes v. Gault*[39] Holmes delivered the opinion of the Court holding that in proceedings for removal of a person under indictment from one federal district to another, the accused was not constitutionally entitled to a hearing and that the statutory implication of a hearing had been satisfied. Brandeis took the position that the Commissioner's refusal to hear certain evidence of the accused going to the issue of probable cause did not merely constitute error but "deprived the petitioner of his liberty without due process of law in violation of the Fifth Amendment, because he was denied a fair hearing." It is worth recalling that in this case the offense for which the accused was indicted was a violation of the antitrust laws, and so we have the spectacle of Holmes, notoriously skeptical of the Sherman Act, lending the aid of the Court to its enforcement, with Brandeis, the friend of antitrust legislation, interposing an obstacle to enforcement. Cases of this sort must trouble those engaged in the occupation of pigeonholing judges. Is this to be classified as an antitrust case, or a criminal case, or forsooth a civil liberties case; and whose was the liberal vote? I leave the answer to those who indulge in the tabulating enterprise.

We return from this digression on Brandeis and Holmes to Brandeis's feeling for the Court as an institution. The sentiment was publicly, though implicitly, reflected in his opinions. They were uniformly addressed to problems and not to persons. They were self-contained, the expression of a judge content to leave his reasoned judgments to the second thought of time and his successors. Not infrequently the preparation of a dissenting opinion was forgone because the demands of other items of work prevented an adequate treatment, but with the promise to himself that another occasion would be taken when circumstances were more propitious. If Brandeis's opinions are firm and poised, it is because they reflect an inner security and confidence and faith in the power of dispassionate reason.

Brandeis was an implicit disciple of Michelangelo: "Take infinite pains to make something that looks effortless." His major opinions went through dozens, sometimes scores, of revisions. He set himself the probably superhuman task of persuading even the losing counsel, and when a petition for rehearing was filed in a case where he had written the opinion, he felt a sense of failure, though I never understood why the intransigence of counsel should be a fault attributable to the judge. Craftsmanship was the best warrant he could give that his work would endure and would be worthy of the immense power and responsibility with which he had been vested.

I have stressed some elements of Brandeis's thought which are apt to be minimized in the popular picture of a liberal judge—his insistence on knowledge, his rejection of opportunism, his insistence on procedural and jurisdictional observances, and his rejection of sentimentality, and in addition, his devotion to the Court while preserving his own intellectual independence. Two other elements in his thinking are also part of his liberalism, but need less emphasis because they are more familiar. I mean, first, his attitude toward *stare decisis*, and second, his expression of economic and social ideas.

It is of course true that he did not regard *stare decisis* as an inexorable command, though he also confessed that "in most matters it is more important that the applicable rule of law be settled than that it be settled right." [40] It was in constitutional cases that he gave freest scope for reconsideration of doctrine, for the only alternative is the heroic process of constitutional amendment. Where the legislature was left free to overcome a decision there was less pressing responsibility on the Court to reconsider, though I do not mean to suggest that he drew a hard and fast line between overruling constitutional doctrine and overruling statutory construction. But it is significant that in one of the most spectacular overrulings of recent years, in *Erie Railroad Company v. Tompkins*,[41] where the century-old precedent of *Swift v. Tyson* was discarded, Brandeis felt impelled to explain that the issues went beyond the mere construction of the Rules of Decision Act of 1790. He ventured to say that the whole course of decision following *Swift v. Tyson*, whereby federal courts had declared the common law independent of state decisions, was unconstitutional. It would have been preferable, I believe, simply to treat the question as one of interpreting the Rules of Decision Act or as one of self-limitation on the part of federal courts in developing the common law. Yet Brandeis's standards of *stare decisis* could not easily be satisfied without putting the matter in terms of re-examining a constitutional question.

The other familiar element in Brandeis's opinions is their employment as a vehicle for his social and economic thought. In the economic area, his essays characteristically took the form of an elucidation of legislative purpose, for he was vindicating the right of experimentation. To be sure, he was an abler exponent than the legislators themselves; they may have marveled at times at the unsuspected depth of their own thinking. Within the confines of the judicial office Brandeis was thus an educator of the first rank. But judges are educators only by the way, as he well knew. It was to education in the general sense, rather than to judges, that he looked for the realization of his hopes for society. In his view, the great depression reflected a failure, not of the law or of the courts or even primarily of economic institutions, but essentially of education. The ill-starred NRA, which he joined in declaring unconstitutional, and whose mistakes were instructive, should have been created, he once remarked, as a bureau in the Office of Education. On a lower level, when he found that more than half of his law clerks were engaged in teaching, he said with satisfaction, "Now I have a majority." His attachment to federalism, a system that was coming into scorn as archaic and obscurantist, had about it an essential feeling for its educational value.[42]

In the area of speech and inquiry, he was, of course, less ready to accept legislative controls on their own terms. What was perhaps his most eloquent opinion was delivered in the case of Anita Whitney, a niece, incidentally, of Justice Field, convicted under a California criminal syndicalism statute for her part in organizing a left-wing party. Urging that the clear-and-present-danger test was the proper criterion in such a case, he argued for the fearless reception of ideas:

> Those who won our independence believed that the final end of the State was to make men free to develop their faculties; and that in its government the deliberative forces should prevail over the arbitrary. They valued liberty both as an end and as a means. They believed liberty to be the secret of happiness and courage to be the secret of liberty. They believed that freedom to think as you will and to speak as you think are means indispensable to the discovery and spread of political truth; that without free speech and assembly discussion would be futile; that with them, discussion affords ordinarily adequate protection against the dissemination of noxious doctrine; that the greatest menace to freedom is an inert people; that public discussion is a political duty; and that this should be a fundamental principle of the American government.[43]

It is hardly necessary to recall that the noble phrase "They believed liberty to be the secret of happiness and courage to be the secret of liberty" is taken straight out of Pericles' funeral oration. (*The Greek Commonwealth*, by Sir Alfred Zimmern, was the book most likely to be recommended by Brandeis to friends in his late years.) But observe the circumspection and caution of Brandeis even in this stirring passage: the circumspection that led him to speak not of the discovery of truth but only of "political" truth, thus averting the shafts leveled by the natural-law philosophers at Holmes; the caution that led him to insert "ordinarily" in relying on discussion as an adequate protection against noxious doctrine. He recognized, in short, that there was a genuine problem here for judges and that not even the eloquence of Pericles could of itself furnish the unfailing answer. The final point to be made is that Brandeis's was a concurring opinion: he joined in the affirmance of Miss Whitney's conviction on the ground that she had not properly raised the issue of clear and present danger in the trial court and hence could not call upon the Supreme Court to pass upon the question. And so Brandeis, who would have wanted to give priority in this case to the mandate for maintaining structure and process over tolerance for legislative experiment, in the end gave primacy to still another principle—the canon of self-limitation. That was still the first mark of the master.

The portrait I have sketched bears little resemblance to the typical picture of the liberal which many hold today. Our age is contentious and frenetic, inclined to distrust the force of standards that one's adversaries may choose to ignore, inclined to seize its own innings and impatiently mark up victories and defeats day by day. And yet who can say that we may safely stake our vision of the future on the accumulation of little triumphs of the day, unless they are earned by what I have ventured to call morality of the mind—by understanding, respect for the limitations as well as the creative opportunities of authority, and the even-handed application of principle? The liberalism of Brandeis the judge was marked by these qualities, and it may have meaning therefore beyond his office and his time—for our day and for the day we shall not see.

★ ★ ★ ★ ★ ★

## VI. JUDGE AND COMPANY

It is notorious that the lawyer has been the most abused of men in the literature of all nations. Perhaps the most compendious abuse was delivered by Plato when he put into the mouth of Socrates these words:

> [The lawyer] is a servant, and is disputing about a fellow-servant before his master, who is seated, and has the cause in his hands; the trial is never about some indifferent matter, but always concerns himself; and often he has to run for his life. The consequence has been, that he has become keen and shrewd; he has learned how to flatter his master in word and indulge him in deed; but his soul is small and unrighteous. His slavish condition has deprived him of growth and uprightness and independence; dangers and fears, which were too much for his truth and honesty, came upon him in early years, when the tenderness of youth was unequal to them, and he has been driven into crooked ways; from the first he has practised

> deception and retaliation, and has become stunted and warped. And so he has passed out of youth into manhood, having no soundness in him; and is now, as he thinks, a master in wisdom. Such is the lawyer, Theodorus.[1]

My interest is with the idea expressed at the beginning of the passage, that the lawyer is a servant disputing before his master seated on the bench. So far as American constitutional law is concerned, it might almost as truly be said that the judge is a servant seated before his masters. The relationship was fairly put, in any case, by Jeremy Bentham when he insisted that the law is not made by judge alone, but by "Judge and Company."

The company who share the lawmaking activity of Supreme Court judges include at least the lower tribunals as well as counsel. The deference paid to the views of other judicial or administrative officers will necessarily be affected by the regard in which they are held. Such deference, as Holmes said of continuity with the past, is not a duty, only a necessity—a psychological necessity. Judge Wyzanski has remarked on the weight that Judge A. N. Hand gave to the opinions of "strong" courts.[2] Lord Bowen, to take the opposite case, is said to have observed, "To have a judgment of my brother Kekewich in your favor is certainly a misfortune, but not necessarily fatal." One may speculate whether the decision in *Betts v. Brady*,[3] holding the appointment of counsel for indigent criminal defendants in state courts not to be an invariable constitutional requirement, would have been the same had the opinion of the court below been written by someone less highly esteemed than Chief Judge Bond of Maryland, who is referred to by name in Mr. Justice Roberts's opinion no fewer than fifteen times. One may speculate, too, whether the decision in the *Japanese Evacuation* cases[4] would have been the same had the final administrative determination been made by someone whose judgment was less deeply respected than Secretary Stimson's.

Of course we are aware of the indebtedness of judges to the briefs and arguments of counsel in the preparation of opinions. Every schoolboy knows how large a part of Daniel Webster's arguments before the Supreme Court found their way into the opinions of Marshall. It seems that Webster was not content to risk his achievement in this regard to the discernment of future historians. He was at pains to point out during his lifetime the extent of his contribution to the judicial utterances of the great Chief Justice. In *Gibbons v. Ogden* Webster was cocounsel with William Wirt, arguing successfully against the New York steamboat monopoly. After the decision, Webster is said to have observed to a friend:

> The opinion of the Court, as rendered by the Chief Justice, was little else than a recital of my argument. The Chief Justice told me that he had little to do but to repeat that argument, as that covered the whole ground. And, which was a little curious, he never referred to the fact that Mr. Wirt had made an argument. He did not speak of it once. . . . That was very singular. It was an accident, I think. Mr. Wirt was a great lawyer, and a great man. But sometimes a man gets a kink and doesn't hit right.[5]

On at least one occasion the argument of Daniel Webster seems to have had a curiously repelling rather than an attracting force with the Court. In the *Rhode Island Rebellion* case, *Luther v. Borden*,[6] Webster represented the officers of the established government who were sued for trespass in putting down the activities of the rival government that the Locofoco party was trying to set up. The argument in the Supreme Court took a broad range. It dealt not only with the principles of representative government but with the place of revolution in our constitutional system. This was certainly strong meat for a court to be asked to chew, and Webster almost at the outset of his argument frankly said so:

> The aspect of the case is, as I have said, novel. It may perhaps give vivacity and variety to judicial investigations. It may relieve the drudgery of perusing briefs, demurrers, and pleas in bar, bills in equity and answers, and introduce topics which give sprightliness, freshness, and something of an uncommon public interest to proceedings in courts of law. . . .
>
> I agree entirely that the case does raise considerations, somewhat extensive, of the true character of our American system of popular liberty; and although I am constrained to differ from the learned counsel who opened the cause for the plaintiff in error, on the principles and character of that American liberty, and upon the true characteristics of that American system on which changes of the government and constitution, if they become necessary, are to be made, yet I agree with him that this case does present them for consideration.[7]

The case of *Luther v. Borden* is now a leading case on what the federal courts will *not* decide. The court regarded the broad questions, so sprightly and fascinating to the student of government, as not within the competence of the judiciary. Whether a purported government is the *de jure* government of a state, and whether it is a representative form of government as guaranteed to the states by the Constitution, are questions that must be left to the other branches of the national government to decide. They are political, not justiciable, questions. It would be tempting to say that Webster had overreached himself in his argument, except for the fact that, in the outcome of the case, his clients prevailed, since the Court professed itself to be in no position to grant relief against the defendant officers.

These are instances in which the dramatic quality of the advocate's argument has played its part. But there are other and subtler ways in which counsel has a crucial role to play in the shaping of constitutional law.

Perhaps the most significant single feature of our system of judicial review of the constitutionality of legislation is the fact that the function is carried out in course of an ordinary lawsuit. The consequence is that many important constitutional questions are decided in litigation that in form is entirely private. The validity of the gold-clause legislation as applied to private debts was decided in a case brought by a bondholder against a railroad on a coupon for $22.50.[8]

The result of this practice has not always been fortunate. Sometimes the Court has decided issues of the gravest importance which it could with propriety have left undecided, and which the judgment of history suggests should have been left for decision at a later date and perhaps by other arbiters. Reference has been made in the first chapter to two cases that Chief Justice Hughes, in his Columbia lectures during his interregnum, referred to as among the Court's self-inflicted wounds—the *Dred Scott* case and the *Income Tax* cases.[9]

These are cases in which counsel were perhaps too eager for the settlement of burning issues. A different sort of danger is also present in such cases—the danger that one side will not have an adequate interest in the presentation of the case. Whether or not a stockholder's suit will produce a real contest, as apparently it did in the *Pollock* case, depends on the attitude of counsel. The Trust Company may be thought not to have had a passionate interest in sustaining the income tax levied upon it, though James C. Carter, who argued for the validity of the tax, had no doubt the greatest personal interest in achieving a victory over his rival at the bar, Joseph H. Choate. Other cases are brought to test the validity of legislation where the element of professional rivalry may not be an adequate safeguard.

One common type of regulation is the prohibition of shipments of certain goods in interstate commerce. A familiar form of litigation under such a statute is a suit by a shipper against a public carrier to compel it to transport the goods. The carrier defends on the ground that the statute forbids the transportation and that the statute is valid.[11] But it may fairly be questioned whether the carrier is deeply interested in sustaining a law that will cut down the volume of goods to be carried.

Whether or not the government was represented at all in these purely private lawsuits depended on whether the government had notice that the suit had been brought, and whether participation as a friend of the court was thought advisable. It was not until 1937 that the government was given a right to become a party in any suit where the constitutionality of an act of Congress was drawn in question. The Judiciary Act of 1937 enables the government not only to present argument to the court, but to participate from the very beginning in the making of the record, so that questions of collusion, lack of standing of the plaintiff, or the relevance of economic and other data to the constitutional issue may be reflected in the record.

The Act of 1937 provides an opportunity for government counsel to make its contribution to the conduct of every case involving the validity of a federal statute. Just what contribution can be made? I shall deal with this question in three aspects—the *what*, the *how*, and the *when* of constitutional litigation.

What the data are upon which the court may draw in deciding a case is largely the responsibility of counsel. Counsel must provide, to use a phrase of Mr. John W. Davis, the implements of decision. Probably the most notable contribution to the lawyer's technique in constitutional cases was the so-called Brandeis brief submitted in the Oregon hours of labor for women case.[12] It drew on reports of public investigating committees, books and articles by medical authorities and social workers, and the practice of legislatures here and abroad. This type of brief has been in fairly common use ever since. It has been particularly utilized by the government. It is one of the few inventions in legal technique that can be identified in a profession that is not notable for wandering off the beaten path. The invention has been widely and justly acclaimed. Yet it raises a number of very real problems, which I shall simply suggest.

In the first place, it may be questioned whether the advocate arguing in favor of the validity of a statute should take the burden of supporting it by a mass of factual data, instead of relying on the presumption of constitutionality. Is not the government advocate who submits a Brandeis brief tempting the court to decide the case without the benefit of the presumption—to decide it, that is, as if the burden of sustaining the statute were upon the proponent? This objection needs to be raised, but it seems to me that it can be answered. The presumption of constitutionality need not be lost sight of; but even a court that relies on the presumption in sustaining a statute does so more confidently and more comfortably if some factual foundation has been established for the validity of the law. And I take it that it is the function of counsel not merely to provide the legal doctrine for deciding the case his way, but to make the court feel comfortable in doing so.

Perhaps a more serious objection to the so-called Brandeis brief is that the data presented ought to be placed in the record and not left simply for the brief. If the data are presented for the record, there will be an opportunity for impeaching them and offering countervailing data. The answer that can be made to this is that the data are offered not for the truth of the facts asserted but only to establish that responsible persons have made the assertions and hold the opinions that are disclosed. The court need not decide, for example, whether filled milk that substitutes coconut oil for butterfat is or is not deceptive or detrimental to health; the court need decide only whether there is responsible opinion that it is so. If there is, the legislation cannot be deemed so arbitrary as to be unconstitutional. The opponents must show—an almost insuperable burden—that the opinion in support of the legislation is wholly untenable. Arguing as counsel in the Oregon minimum wage case, Brandeis put the point in extreme terms:

> In answer to the question, whether this brief contains also all the data opposed to minimum-wage law, I want to say this: I conceive it to be absolutely immaterial what may be said against such laws. Each one of these statements contained in the brief in support of the contention that this is wise legislation, might upon further investigation be found to be erroneous, each conclusion of fact may be found afterwards to be unsound—and yet the constitutionality of the act would not be affected thereby. This court is not burdened with the duty of passing upon the disputed question whether the legislature of Oregon was wise or unwise, or probably wise or unwise, in enacting this law. The question is merely whether, as has been stated, you can see that the legislators had no ground on which they could, as reasonable men, deem this legislation appropriate to abolish or mitigate the evils believed to exist or apprehended. If you cannot find that, the law must stand.[13]

In the light of this rationale, the use made by the Court in the school desegregation cases of sociological writings is open to question—though, it should be added at once, the professional sociologists notwithstanding, such data were not crucial to the result. These writings were employed not to support the reasonableness of the legislative judgment but to overturn it. Their use would be compatible with the theory of the Brandeis brief only if the usual presumption in favor of legislation is reversed in cases of racial classification—a proposition not explicitly set forth by the Court.

In any event, whatever the type of case, there is much to be said for providing an opportunity in the trial court to impeach or controvert the expert opinion that is relied on. Indeed, it should be said that the practice of the government and other litigants has by no means been limited to the placing of such data in the briefs. In many of the most important constitutional cases, the material has actually been introduced into the record. Sometimes this has been done by calling expert witnesses—government economists or outside economists—or by introducing into the record publications of responsible authorities. This was done, for example, in the Guffey Coal Act case,[14] where voluminous testimony was taken regarding the history of labor disturbances in the coal industry and the effect on the volume of shipments and competitive conditions in the industry. It was done in the *PWA* cases,[15] where testimony was taken regarding studies made by the Bureau of Labor Statistics on the effectiveness of a public works program in the relief of unemployment. It was done at great length in the omnibus *TVA* case,[16] where a galaxy of engineers—military, civil, and hydraulic—testified on both sides concerning the usefulness of the TVA projects for navigation, flood control, and national defense.

One final objection to the so-called Brandeis brief is that it places an inappropriate task on counsel. Is the adversary method the most suitable one for dealing with economic data? Someone has said that there are three sides to every lawsuit—my side, your side, and the truth. Should the responsibility for developing the background facts be placed on counsel, or should it be borne by some disinterested source? Should there be established for the courts something equivalent to the legislative reference service organized in a number of states for the benefit of the legislature? This would perhaps be a more radical innovation than the Brandeis brief itself, and yet it is not altogether fanciful. We owe much of our commercial law to the boldness of Lord Mansfield in seeking advice from experienced merchants regarding mercantile practices. The English admiralty courts have utilized the services of retired mariners drawn from the Royal Navy and the Merchant Marine—the celebrated "elder brethren of Trinity House." Some of our courts are beginning to employ disinterested medical and psychiatric advisers. The great difficulty with this idea in constitutional litigation is that the experts would be tempted to intrude their views on the merits of the legislation instead of helping the court to understand other people's views. Perhaps the right place for non-legal-experts in constitutional law is in the legislative process. If records of hearings and committee reports, particularly in state legislatures, were more illuminating and accessible, the task of the advocate in court would be simpler, and the court itself would be more disposed to display that basic judicial virtue, humility.

When we pass from *what* is presented to *how* it is presented, the role of counsel is even more striking. To some degree, the choice of the lawsuit that is to be the test case is in counsel's hands. Should a case be chosen which will present the issues narrowly or broadly? Should an all-out contest be risked or should a more limited engagement be fought?

The long-drawn-out litigation over the TVA was a clash of two views of constitutional warfare. The power companies endeavored to attack what they described as the whole "plan and program" of the TVA, as revealed in speeches, official studies, and promotional literature dealing with the development of a great river system and electrification of the valley. One of these documents to which the power companies were fond of pointing bore the lyrical title "There'll be Shouting in the Valley." The TVA, on the other hand, insisted that all that was in issue in the case was the lawfulness of certain hydroelectric structures already completed and the sale of power under contracts already in existence or definitely contemplated. The first case was in form a stockholders' suit by preferred stockholders against the Alabama Power Company and the TVA to enjoin the performance of a contract the company had made with the Authority. The company was controlled by Commonwealth & Southern, which owned all the common stock and which had arranged for the contract—or truce, as it was sometimes called—with the TVA. This accounts for the fact that the suit was begun by preferred rather than by common stockholders. The contract provided for the sale of transmission lines to the TVA, and a division of territory between the company and TVA in Alabama. All the electric energy the TVA would need in order to serve the territory ceded to it by the company in Alabama could be supplied by the generators at Wilson Dam. That dam was begun in 1918 and completed in 1925, long before the New Deal and TVA came upon the scene. In fact, it was authorized originally as a military project to provide power for the manufacture of nitrates. As I have said, the counsel for the complainants regarded the case as one to test the whole plan and policy of the TVA. Counsel for the TVA maintained that what was in issue was simply the validity of Wilson Dam and the contractual arrangement for the sale of power from that dam to municipalities in the area.

The district court granted a broad injunction against the TVA, with numerous findings and conclusions regarding the development of the entire Tennessee River as contemplated under the TVA Act. But the court made a finding, fatal to its own conception of the case, that Wilson Dam would supply all the power necessary to serve the customers in the territory formerly served by the Alabama Power Company. That finding became of critical importance on appeal. When Chief Justice Hughes asked counsel for the Power Company what the precise issue in the case was, counsel replied that it was the plan and program of the TVA; whereupon the Chief Justice said: "It is the validity of a contract, is it not?" With that definition of the issue, the result of the case was hardly in doubt. The lawfulness of Wilson Dam was sustained under the government's war powers and the power over commerce on navigable waters, and the purchase of transmission lines for the sale of power from the Dam was sustained as a legitimate means of disposing of government-owned property—that is, the water power that is inevitably created by the maintenance of the Dam and the flow of water over it.[17] There is a treasure in the waters, as government counsel put it, and the Constitution does not require that it go to waste.

This was, of course, only the preliminary skirmish, though it seemed to lay the groundwork for upholding the dams constructed under TVA auspices, with their generators and transmission lines. The strategy and counterstrategy became more subtle. The power companies now made sure that they would have a case presenting the TVA program in its broadest scope. They brought together nineteen companies, serving the southeastern United States, in a huge omnibus suit challenging all phases of the TVA power activities. This suit took a curious course before it was finally decided in the Supreme Court. As a matter of fact, it started out, not as one, but as two identical suits. One was filed in the federal court for northern Alabama and the other in a state court in Tennessee. They were identical bills of complaint and were filed on the same day. This maneuver reflected uncertainty regarding venue. The TVA statute provides that the legal residence of the TVA is at Muscle Shoals, Alabama. Doubtless counsel for the power companies feared that suit would have to be brought in Alabama, or at least that a suit elsewhere would run the risk of eventual dismissal on venue or jurisdictional grounds. Nevertheless, the power companies were anxious to try a forum other than Alabama and the Fifth Circuit, where the Court of Appeals had ruled adversely to them in the stockholders' case. Their plan evidently was to retain the Alabama suit simply as an anchor to windward while actively pursuing the Tennessee suit. The TVA met these tactics by attempting to bring on the Alabama suit for a prompt hearing on a motion to dismiss the bill of complaint, while filing an answer and moving slowly in the Tennessee case.

At this juncture the power companies decided to dismiss the Alabama suit voluntarily rather than risk its becoming the test case, and so they staked everything on the Tennessee proceeding, trusting that it would not be dismissed for lack of jurisdiction. They had very adroitly brought it in a state court in Tennessee, thus forcing the TVA to take the initiative in removing it to a federal court. By removing it, the TVA was barred from objecting in the federal court that the venue of the action was not properly laid in Tennessee. The TVA had one countermove, which was ingenious but inadequate. Though objection to venue was lost by removal, lack of "jurisdiction" of the state court could still be set up, for the jurisdiction of a federal court on removal is derivative. The TVA argued that under Tennessee law an action against a public agency could be brought only in the courts of the agency's legal headquarters, which would be Alabama in this case. Had this argument been effective, the companies, which had deliberately instituted the case in the state rather than federal court in order to force a waiver of venue, would have been hoist by their own petard. Unfortunately for the cause of poetic justice, but I daresay properly, the Tennessee law was held not to support the TVA's argument *in extremis*.

The result of all these maneuvers was that the case was finally established in a federal court in Tennessee before a single judge. He granted a sweeping preliminary injunction against TVA; the TVA appealed to the circuit court of appeals. That court reversed the preliminary injunction and sent the case back for trial.[18] Meanwhile, however, Congress and the President had been wrestling with the so-called reorganization of the federal judiciary, less politely known as the court-packing plan. That plan, of course, never became law, but out of it grew the Judiciary Act of 1937, which contained a provision that a three-judge court must be called when an injunction is sought against the enforcement of a federal statute on constitutional grounds. By the time the TVA case was remanded to the trial court, this provision was in force, and hence the district court judge who granted the injunction now found himself flanked by two associates. After a lengthy trial, the three-judge court ruled in favor of the TVA, with some adverse findings by the judge who had first sat in the case.

It is always tempting to look back on history and speculate on what would have happened to the face of the world if Cleopatra's nose had been half an inch longer, or if the Germans had kept their right flank stronger in the drive on Paris in 1914. If the power companies had not asked for a preliminary injunction, there would have been no basis for an intermediate appeal, and the case might have been tried before the single judge and decided finally by him in favor of the power companies, with appropriate findings before the three-judge-court provision was enacted into law. At any rate, the companies were defeated in the three-judge court and appealed to the Supreme Court. The TVA maintained throughout the case that the power companies had no standing to object to competition, whether the TVA, in the abstract, was or was not constitutional. In the Supreme Court it was this defense that prevailed.[19] Thus technically the Supreme Court did not give us a decision on the validity of the entire TVA power program. Yet I cannot help believing that the detailed findings of the three-judge court in support of the validity of the TVA as a co-ordinated navigation, flood control, and hydroelectric project made it more comfortable for the Supreme Court to dismiss the power companies' case on what might appear to be somewhat technical grounds.

The TVA litigation is only one illustration of jockeying for position in constitutional lawsuits. An even more vivid instance occurred in the holding-company litigation. The interests opposed to the Holding Company Act were anxious to secure as early as possible a sweeping decision declaring the whole scheme of regulation unconstitutional. They were on the alert for a case that would lend itself to this purpose. The government, on the other hand, and in particular the Securities and Exchange Commission, which had the responsibility of administering the Act, was anxious to confine the first case under the Act to the question of the duty of utilities to register with the Commission. The other provisions of the Act, the so-called control provisions—relating to issuance of securities, acquisition of property, intercorporate loans, simplification of holding-company structure, and the like—would thus be left for decision as cases should arise in the course of actions taken by the SEC against particular companies. The SEC, moreover, was anxious that the first case should involve a relatively large and representative system, so that the practices that led to the enactment of the statute could be fully and fairly presented.

The utilities believed that they had found a case suitable in all respects for their purposes in the bankruptcy proceedings involving a relatively small holding-company in the Maryland federal court.[20] One possibility of a quick and broad decision, without the hindrance of having the government as a party to the suit (for this was prior to the 1937 act), was simply that the trustee in bankruptcy might ask the court for instructions regarding the validity of the Act in order to receive directions whether or not to comply. In a similar case in the Delaware federal court, Judge Nields refused to give such instructions, stating that it was an attempt to secure a decision striking down an act of Congress in the absence of those who were responsible for administering it.[21] Such a course, he said, would violate accepted canons of judicial procedure. To be sure, such constitutional decisions had frequently been given in the absence of government representation; but here there was the special factor that the case did not seem to contain the safeguards of an adversary proceeding.

In the Maryland case, counsel were more careful. They took pains to see that there would be adverse claims made in the bankruptcy proceedings with respect to the validity of the statute. One bondholder, a corporation owning $150,000 in first lien bonds of the debtor, took the position that its interest would best be served by an outright liquidation of the company. It maintained that the Holding Company Act would require a liquidation because no reorganization of the system would be possible under the simplification provisions of the statute. Consequently, its counsel was in the position of arguing for the validity of the statute. The opposing side was taken in an intervening petition by another creditor, who owned $2,500 in bonds of the debtor. He agreed that the Holding Company Act would require liquidation and prevent reorganization; but he alleged that he desired a reorganization. His interest, therefore, was in having the statute declared unconstitutional.

At this juncture the Securities and Exchange Commission, through its counsel, came on the scene and urged the district court not to pass on the constitutional questions in this proceeding. It argued that such a decision would be premature, since the time for registration had not yet arrived and the Commission had taken no action regarding the company; that the facts concerning this holding-company system were not adequately disclosed in the agreed statement; that counsel on both sides had joined in construing the Holding Company Act as preventing reorganization, a doubtful construction, which the Commission should have an opportunity to consider in administrative proceedings relating to this company; and finally, that it did not appear that the interests of the respective creditors were genuinely adverse. The circumstances surrounding the intervention of the creditor holding $2,500 in bonds and attacking the validity of the statute were disclosed when he was subpoenaed and examined by counsel for the SEC. It turned out that he was a dentist who had bought the securities through a local brokerage office, and his broker had asked him to sign the document that constituted the intervening petition. The circumstances are best revealed in his testimony:

A. He simply called me up and said that there was a reorganization taking place, or they wanted to reorganize the company and wanted to know if I would sign some papers in regard to it. That is all I know.
Q. Did he describe the papers to you?
A. No, sir, he said he would bring them up.
Q. Did he tell you who was going to be your lawyer?
A. I think he said something about a Mr. Davis being in town representing the company.
Q. Representing the company?
A. Yes.
Q. Did he say that Mr. Davis was going to represent you?
A. No, sir.
Q. And you have never met Mr. Davis?
A. No, sir.
Q. Nor Mr. Piper?
A. No, sir.
Q. And where was this petition which you signed, when was it signed?
A. I judge about a week ago, a week or ten days ago. I paid no particular attention to the date.
Q. Where did you sign it?

A. Down in the attorney's office. . . .
Q. Well, tell the circumstances of your signing it.
A. I asked why I was called to sign it, and after I signed it they sort of smiled and said, Well, you are the only one in Baltimore owned any of it.
Q. And did you know the contents of that petition?
A. I read it.
Q. Well, did you appreciate the contents of it?
A. As best that I could. I could not remember it now.
Q. Could you or not give your judgment as to what was in the paper that you signed?
A. Just something that they wanted to reorganize the company whereby they could realize something out of it. Otherwise, the way I understand it, the Government was trying to confiscate the holding company or something of that kind.
Q. You don't know the circumstances of the—you don't recall the particular allegation in the petition?
A. I can not say that I do.
Q. And was it explained to you that the Government was going to confiscate the property of the utilities?
A. No, that is the way I understood it.
Q. Was any explanation given of the nature of this paper? . . .
A. No. The paper was simply brought up to me and [they] asked me to sign it. I said, You are asking me to sign something I haven't had a chance to read, I would like to read it. I thought it was my duty to sign it, and therefore I signed the paper. According to the contents of it it sounded logical to me.
Q. Did you have an appreciation that at that time you were being represented by Mr. Davis of New York?
A. Not I, personally, no.
Q. You have never met Mr. Davis personally?
A. I don't know the gentleman.
Q. You never made any arrangements to pay any attorney any fee for representing you?
A. No, sir.

Q. You never made any arrangements to retain an attorney to act for you personally in your interests?

A. No, sir.[22]

On cross-examination, the witness agreed to be represented by the designated counsel.[23]

The district court refused to dismiss or delay the proceedings and rendered a decision declaring the entire statute unconstitutional.[24] This decision was affirmed by the circuit court of appeals.[25] Both sides, that is, the two creditors, joined in asking the Supreme Court to take the case on certiorari in order that a prompt decision could be had. At this point government counsel made a last effort to prevent this case from being the vehicle for a decision on the validity of the Act. The government filed a memorandum in the Supreme Court as a friend of the court urging the inappropriateness of the case and asking that certiorari be denied. The Supreme Court denied certiorari.[26] Thus the campaign to make this the test case finally failed.

Meanwhile the government was besieged with dozens of injunction suits scattered over the country brought by utility companies to restrain the enforcement of the Act prior to the date for registration. In order to hold these cases in abeyance, the government took defensive action. All government officers who might have had authority to take steps toward the enforcement of the Act were instructed to do nothing pending a decision by the Supreme Court in a test case. The Postmaster General so instructed local postmasters with respect to their power over the mails; the Attorney General so instructed United States attorneys with respect to their power to commence criminal proceedings; and the SEC itself disclaimed any intention to enforce the statute until a test of the registration provisions could be had. In order to encourage the companies to register and to contest specific applications of the Act later if they were so inclined, the Commission announced that registration would not waive any constitutional objections that might subsequently be raised, and that if any court should hold that registration was a waiver, the registration should be considered to be rescinded. The most serious of the injunction suits were those in the District of Columbia, where jurisdiction could be had over the members of the Commission. In these suits, the Attorney General took the unusual course of appearing in the district court and himself arguing for a stay order until a case that meanwhile was brought in the federal court in New York could be decided. The New York case was planned by the SEC as the test case; it involved the Electric Bond & Share Company and was a proceeding to compel it to register, with the company filing a cross bill asking that the Act as a whole and its various control provisions in particular be declared unconstitutional. The District of Columbia court granted a stay in the cases pending before it, and with some modification of its terms, the stay order was approved by the Supreme Court.[27] So at last the way was cleared for the test case, which in due course wound its way from the district court in New York through the circuit court of appeals and to the Supreme Court, and which resulted in a decision upholding the registration provisions of the Act and declining to pass on the so-called control provisions.[28]

Both here and in the *TVA* cases the basic contest was over the scope of the issues. If the government could keep the case within a relatively narrow compass, it could confidently expect success. The opposition staked its chances on opening up the statutes to the widest possible attack before the government had a chance to settle down to the task of administering them. The fate of the statutes may well have turned on *how* the constitutional questions were presented.

The "how" of constitutional litigation shades off into the "when," or perhaps I should say the "whether." The timing of constitutional litigation may be of critical importance. Should the determination of constitutional issues be postponed or expedited? This raises questions of policy that affect the Court, the government, and the public. Traditionally, the Court professes never to decide a constitutional question unless and until it is necessary to the decision of an actual controversy. I have suggested that when the Court has departed from this principle, it has sometimes produced, in Hughes's phrase, self-inflicted wounds. The fallibility of judges, and the enormously difficult task of overcoming an adverse decision through constitutional amendment, as well as the possibility of working a change in the law through the political processes, all indicate the wisdom of the policy of "sufficient unto the day is the evil thereof." This, however, requires some qualification. In the case of laws that interfere with freedom of expression or other civil and political rights, the channels of orderly change are by hypothesis clogged, and intervention by the Court at an early stage has some special justification, provided that the operation of the law in question can be actually delineated.

From the standpoint of those charged with administering the laws, there can be no generalization regarding the wisdom of delay or expedition in constitutional cases, nor has there been any general practice in this regard. The *Gold Clause* cases were expedited to the limit; in one of the cases the government petitioned for certiorari prior to argument of the case in the circuit court of appeals, and the petition was granted despite the fact that the government, seeking review, had been the successful party in the district court.[29] In the *Social Security* cases, the time elapsed between the bringing of the cases and the final decision in the Supreme Court was a matter only of months.[30] On the other hand, the government made no effort to secure an early decision on the NIRA, and in fact, on the eve of argument in the Supreme Court dismissed a case that it had appealed and that seemed destined to be the test case.[31] And in the TVA and holding-company litigations, as we have seen, the government was more anxious that the right case be decided than that a case be decided early.

These differences are not the result of pure caprice. They depend on a number of factors. Does the law look toward administrative case-by-case application? The Gold Clause legislation operated of its own force without implementation. This was not true of the Holding Company Act. How serious will be the uncertainty pending a decision? Uncertainty regarding the social security legislation meant uncertainty regarding a major item in the budget. It is true that uncertainty regarding the NIRA helped to undermine its administration, but it was doubtless felt that this incident of delay was outweighed by the fact that the statute could best be judged by examining its application to specific industries in specific codes, and the fact that in any event the statute was to expire two years after its enactment, and Congress was entitled to learn from its own mistakes before learning from the Supreme Court. And it would be less than candid not to add that an appraisal of the temper of the Court plays its part. And so the question whether to use Fabian tactics or push for a quick decision is a major problem of policy for government counsel. In resolving the problem, the public interest must not be overlooked. Uncertainty regarding Gold Clause legislation meant uncertainty in countless day-to-day business transactions. Uncertainty regarding the TVA and the Holding Company Act caused inconvenience to a smaller though substantial number of people; but the adverse effect of the acts on those concerned was not so certain.

The order in which cases are brought is often of first importance. As we are reminded by Edgar in *King Lear*, Ripeness is all. Or, to change the figure, it is easier to establish a proposition of law in two jumps than in one. It was easier to hold that Congress could prohibit outright the interstate shipment of goods made by child labor after the Court had held that Congress could prohibit the interstate shipment of prison-made goods into states that prohibit the local sale of such goods.[32] The fact that the Congressional policy was tied in to the local policy was a bridge that helped in crossing the constitutional gap; and when once the crossing had been made, it was possible for the Court to burn the bridge behind it. It was the policy of taking two steps instead of one that largely accounted for the government's action in dismissing in the Supreme Court the Louisville slum clearance case, which would have tested the power of eminent domain in aid of spending for the general welfare.[33] At that time, the general welfare clause had not been authoritatively construed, and it was felt that the question of eminent domain ought to await the decision of a case involving simply the spending power without any question of compulsory taking of property. The tactics here employed resemble somewhat the military tactics that Marshal Foch is said to have urged on young officers. He advised them to watch the movement of a parrot in its cage, which progresses by reaching out one claw, grasping firmly, and pausing before bringing the other claw into position—grasp, pause, grasp, pause, was his description of successful forward movement, and whatever its application to modern warfare, it is not a bad motto for constitutional litigation.

The opportunity that government counsel enjoys of planning and timing, within limits, the sequence of litigation, carries with it a corresponding responsibility of consistency and candor. It was decided in the mid-nineteen-thirties, with approval on the highest administrative level, to move toward an end of intergovernmental tax immunities for private taxpayers.[34] Government counsel initiated the movement by arguing as *amicus curiae* that the states have power to tax contractors on federal projects on their gross receipts, including sums received from the government.[35] This was a notable piece of self-denial, since costs to the government might be increased by reason of these taxes. But the problem was a reciprocal one, and later the government was able consistently to argue for the validity of a federal tax on salaries of state employees, and still later, and consistently, as *amicus curiae* for the validity of a state tax on salaries of federal employees.[36] But having displayed this degree of disinterestedness, the Department of Justice came under great pressure from budget-conscious departments to reassert the doctrine of immunity for contractors under cost-plus arrangements with the government, and when counsel yielded to the pressure the government was rebuffed by the Court.[37] The momentum of the government's march was not to be stopped at its will. Mr. Justice Roberts subsequently observed pointedly that "the Government repented its generosity." [38]

Of course there are circumstances when counsel cannot safely abandon a position of protecting the pecuniary interests of their client, the Federal Treasury, until the Supreme Court speaks. On one occasion the government was taxing certain transfers under the gift tax as completed gifts, or under the estate tax as transfers to take effect at death, depending on the advantages to the Treasury in each case, pending clarification of the issue by the Supreme Court. Companion cases reached the Court, in which the government had taken contradictory legal positions. They were argued in succession by the same counsel for the government, who insisted in the one that the transfer was a completed gift and with equal earnestness in the other that the same kind of transfer was testamentary. This understandably perplexed counsel for the second taxpayer, who complained to the Court that the government's argument had straddled the fence. Chief Justice Hughes interposed, "I should say rather that Miss Carloss has managed to alight gracefully on both sides of the fence."

Candor has impelled counsel for the government to confess error in a substantial number of cases reaching the Supreme Court on the opponent's petition. Sometimes the government is more royalist than the King, and its exercise of a judicious temperament is met by a resistant Court, which refuses to agree that the government's case is hopeless. On one occasion a member of the Court was heard to complain that he thought "the Court is entitled to more advocacy from the Government." In the long run, candor is not simply its own reward. Mr. Justice Holmes once complimented a solicitor general on his candor before the Court. As the Solicitor General was drawing himself up in satisfaction, Holmes added: "You know, candor is one of the most effective instruments in deception."

What can be said of the role of counsel in constitutional litigation in the future? Government counsel will, of course, retain in delicate balance its threefold responsibility—to the Court, to the administrative agencies, and to the public. Counsel for both government and private interests will do well to heed the lesson that the reach must not exceed the grasp. Declaratory judgments and broad injunctions are tempting, but those seeking them are frequently left empty handed. It is sounder to argue a constitutional case as a case, arguing for victory on constitutional grounds if need be, but above all arguing the case and not an abstract question of constitutional law. This does not mean that constitutional questions should be ignored in the early stages of the case. On the contrary, counsel may find that unless they have raised the questions at an early stage, so that the lower court is called on to consider them, the Supreme Court will refuse to pass on them. Constitutional questions should be envisaged at the earliest possible stage in the litigation, and should be appropriately raised by pleadings and evidence; but they should not be developed to the exclusion of other issues on which the case may be decided.

The Supreme Court's recent reluctance to declare state laws unconstitutional under the due process clause unless basic civil liberties are involved has important implications for litigation. The result may well be that constitutional litigation over state laws will be concentrated more and more in state courts under state constitutional provisions, and state constitutional law may become of dominant importance. In the field of federal legislation, the constitutional issues may be increasingly diverted from the federal courts to the legislative stage, so that the constitutional lawyer's function will be discharged more frequently before Congressional committees than in court. Constitutional law may thus become one phase of legislative drafting. This centering of constitutional debate is salutary, subject to two cautions: the constitutional validity of a bill must not be taken to resolve questions of its wisdom, and per contra, some residual constitutional doubts about a bill should not necessarily debar its passage, especially when the measure will be subject to judicial review and the doubts may be resolved by the administration of the law. The legislature has to reach a final collective judgment on the merits of proposed legislation; in most instances it does not have to pass finally on constitutionality.

And so in finding a role for "Judge and Company" in constitutional law, we are led back to our starting point, to the place of the Court in the complex of government. We have arrived full circle at the problem of the One and the Many.

# VII. THE COURT AND ITS CRITICS

Sixty-three years ago Mr. Justice Brewer, a judge who was hardly the darling of the forces of democracy, had this to say about the role of criticism of the Supreme Court:

> It is a mistake to suppose that the Supreme Court is either honored or helped by being spoken of as beyond criticism. On the contrary, the life and character of its justices should be the objects of constant watchfulness by all, and its judgments subjected to the freest criticism. . . . True, many criticisms may be, like their authors, devoid of good taste, but better all sorts of criticism than no criticism at all.[1]

Americans have not been reticent about availing themselves of this privilege. From John Marshall's day onward a tide of critical commentary has run—of varying degrees of respectfulness and respectability. Even state judges have at times joined the ranks of the critics; human nature being what it is, a judge who is reversed on appeal is likely to be of the same opinion still. Chief Justice Roane of Virginia, for example, could write of an opinion of Marshall's: ". . . a most monstrous and unexampled decision. It can only be accounted for by that love of power which history informs us infects and corrupts all who possess it, and from which even the upright and eminent judges are not exempt." [2] Since the state chief justices had not then formed themselves into a corporate body one of whose functions is to vote in review of its reviewer, historians have to be content with the individual and personal observations of judicial critics of the past.

Today all criticism of the Court runs the risk of fanning the fires of lawlessness and cynicism that have been ignited in the wake of the school desegregation cases. As the school cases have been the precipitating cause of these current onslaughts, it is right that any general assessment of the Court should not ignore those decisions. A sense of responsibility would seem to require no less. Consequently, I will venture to rethresh this straw before proceeding to greener pastures. If what I say is a thrice-told tale, my excuse can be drawn from the always comforting advice of Mr. Justice Holmes that we need education in the obvious more than investigation of the obscure.

The first obvious fact is that the Court did not inject itself into the issue of school desegregation; the issue was put before it inescapably. One may agree or disagree with the tactics that led the parents and their advisers to press the issue when they did, but the choice of time or of priorities did not lie within the control of the Court. Its choice was only how to decide; and in appraising the decisions and their aftermath, we must compare, not the present condition and that existing before 1954, but the present condition and that which would have come about had the decisions gone the other way—had the Court ruled that the constitutional guarantee of equal protection of the laws is satisfied by a law that classifies applicants for admission to a public school not on the basis of individual fitness but on the basis of color. It is proving very hard indeed in some quarters to live physically with the Court's decisions; would it not have proved even harder to live intellectually and morally with a contrary decision?

The next obvious fact is that the Court recognized the genuine problems of transition that would be encountered in some localities and for that reason rejected the urging of the petitioners and the Department of Justice that a definite time limit be fixed for plans of compliance. Instead, the Court took the more moderate course of setting the standard of deliberate speed, a standard that would surely allow adaptation to local conditions, provided always that a bona fide use of time was made to bring about ultimate desegregation. Here was an opportunity for American federalism to demonstrate its creative powers, its talent for diversity within unity, its experimental gift for devising a plurality of ways to a common goal. Not the least of the tragedies of the situation is that the energies of our federal process should be employed in the ingenuities of evasion instead of the resourcefulness of compliance.

A final obvious fact is that the decisions were not an abrupt departure in constitutional law or a novel interpretation of the guarantee of equal protection of the laws. The old doctrine of separate-but-equal, announced in 1896, had been steadily eroded for at least a generation before the school cases, in the way that precedents are whittled down until they finally collapse.

Two episodes will illustrate the process. The first occurred in 1917, and turned on the validity of a Louisville ordinance that provided for racial zoning.[3] The avowed purpose of the ordinance, as set forth in its title, has a familiar ring: "An Ordinance to Prevent

Conflict and Ill-Feeling Between the White and Colored Races in the City of Louisville, and to Preserve the Public Peace and Promote the General Welfare by Making Reasonable Provisions Requiring as Far as Practicable, the Use of Separate Blocks for Residences, Places of Abode, and Places of Assembly by White and Colored People Respectively." To this the answer was made in a brief *amicus curiae* filed by two distinguished St. Louis lawyers, one of them, Frederick W. Lehmann, a former solicitor general and as powerful a one as we have had. They said:

> [The ordinance] cannot be justified by the recitals of the title, even if they are true. Many things may rouse a man's prejudice or stir him to anger, but he is not always to be humored in his wrath. The question may arise, "Dost thou well to be angry?"

The relevance of the separate-but-equal doctrine for transportation and schools to the problem of separate residential areas was not lost on counsel for the city. It argued in its brief, in a passage that now has a certain wry humor, that:

> . . . precisely the same facts which make it wise to separate children and adults in the schools exist for separating them as immediate neighbors. *If there is danger of conflict, and of peril to the preservation of the purity of the race, where there is merely the brief and temporary and almost casual association in the schools and in the vehicles of public travel, how much greater must be this same danger where the relation is the fixed and permanent and uninterrupted one of immediate neighbors on the same block; the negro with his family living side by side with the white man's family, day after day and year after year?* [Italics in original.]

This argument was unavailing in the Supreme Court of 1917.

The second episode occurred in 1938, and turned on the plan of Missouri to provide for the legal education of Negroes by paying their expenses in a law school in a neighboring state. Again the plan was upset by the Court, in a decision whose implications were not lost on Mr. Justice McReynolds, dissenting. He wrote:

> For a long time Missouri has acted upon the view that the best interest of her people demands separation of whites and negroes in schools. Under the opinion just announced, I presume she may abandon her law school and thereby disadvantage her white citizens without impairing petitioner's opportunities for legal instruction; or she may break down the settled practice concerning separate schools and thereby, as indicated by experience, damnify both races.[4]

It is, of course, dangerous to accept a dissenting opinion as an objective guide to the meaning of a decision. But in this instance Mr. Justice McReynolds saw which way the winds of doctrine were blowing, and he did not like what he saw. What he beheld was a steady, unmistakable progression on the part of the Court in applying the guarantee of equal protection of the laws to a sequence of issues: the right to serve on juries, the right to vote in primaries, the right to choose a place of residence without a legal color bar, the right to be considered for admission to a state professional school without discrimination because of race. The Court was recognizing the developing consciousness of the country that equal protection of the laws was to be given a full and not a qualified meaning. Each of these stages was marked by vigorous and sincere protest and by local resistance. The school cases differ from these precedents primarily in the fact that escape from the school decisions is much more difficult because attendance at the public school is an open, notorious, and everyday activity. Consequently, it is at the present stage in this steady advance that we are seeing what Alfred North Whitehead described in his study of symbolism:

> It is the first step in sociological wisdom to recognize that the major advances in civilization are processes which all but wreck the societies in which they occur—like unto an arrow in the hand of a child. The art of free society consists first in the maintenance of the symbolic code; and secondly in fearlessness of revision, to secure that the code serves those purposes which satisfy an enlightened reason. Those societies which cannot combine reverence to their symbols with freedom of revision, must ultimately decay either from anarchy, or from the slow atrophy of a life stifled by useless shadows.[5]

It is most certainly not the function of the Court to intensify these explosive pressures. It is the function of the Court to moderate, in the double sense of deciding and ameliorating. The Court has been most successful in its tasks, whether in the maintenance of state-federal relations or in the realm of civil liberties, when it has avoided commitment to absolutes and has worked out an accommodation of interests. It is one of the virtues of the litigation process that, because of the complexity and the richness of the strands of experience which are caught up in the pattern of litigation, absolute and intransigent positions are moderated through the process of judicial decision. In the school cases this was done, as I have suggested, through the form of the decree, which was an appeal to the resources of federalism to work out a viable solution within the framework of the principle of desegregation. If the ingenuity and energy spent on resistance were to be expended on devising ways of compliance, and if the collaborative efforts of white citizens' councils were to be matched by collaboration with those who have successfully administered a changeover from segregated to desegregated schools, the problem would yield to reason, good will, and practical sense.

One thing is certain—ignorant and disgraceful billingsgate will not bring about a change in judicial action. What it will do is stimulate a spirit of lawlessness and bigotry, evidences of which we are already seeing in more than one part of the country and in more than one area of American life.

There are other and subtler consequences of the irresponsible attacks on the Court. For one thing, as we weaken the habit of respect for law and legal institutions, we disqualify ourselves for leadership in the movement—groping and fragile as it is—toward a common law of mankind. The atmosphere of cynicism and lawlessness is a fallout that not only contaminates our own lives, but by spreading a pall over our aspirations for a regime of world law, poisons our own and the world's future as well.

A final and ironic consequence of unbridled criticism is that all other criticism may be inhibited, lest it be seized on and distorted into a weapon in the warfare being waged against the Court. It would be a great disservice if it came to pass that the only alternatives open to observers of the Court were unbridled abuse or indiscriminate praise. To avoid this dilemma, a critique of the Court must possess that quality of judiciousness which is demanded of the Court itself. Criticism should be informed by perspective and infused by philosophy.

It will be convenient to consider the current criticisms of the Court in three aspects: the Court's review of other agencies of Government; its attitude toward its own jurisdiction; and its craftsmanship.

One starts naturally with the criticism leveled by the report of the State Chief Justices in 1958. There is a piquant quality about the judges voting in review of their reviewer—like the tailor retailored or the biter bit. Their critique admonished the Court of the virtue of self-restraint, and in particular, deplored what they regarded as a whittling down of state powers. Among the principal cases to which the report pointed an accusing finger were those on antisubversion laws of the states, decisions on admission to the bar, review of state criminal convictions, and oversight of legislative investigations. In all of these fields the Supreme Court has had occasion in recent years to reverse state court decisions or to invalidate state action. I shall turn to these cases presently. At this point it is pertinent to notice some matters on which the report of the state judges had little to say.

The areas of state authority with which state officials may be most legitimately concerned are really three: state regulation, state taxation, and political self-determination on the part of a state. In each of these fields the Supreme Court over the past twenty years has shown a marked degree of self-restraint. Indeed the greatest contrast between the modern Court and its immediate predecessors is in the deference that is now paid to social and economic measures enacted by the states.[6] Similarly, in the field of taxation, state measures that would have run afoul of the judicial veto a generation ago, because of doctrines of burden on interstate commerce or intergovernmental immunities, have now been sustained.[7] And in the political realm, perhaps the most critical issue is the autonomy of the state with regard to its pattern of elected representatives, that is, its pattern of legislative districting. Here, despite vigorous protest both without the Court and from a minority within, the Court has declined to review the action of state legislatures in setting up grossly unequal local and Congressional districts.[8] Any balanced assessment of the Court's intervention in local affairs as against its exercise of self-restraint must surely give great weight to the abstention of the Court in all these central fields of state activity.

It is in the field of speech and assembly and free exercise of religion, together with procedural due process, that the modern Court has been most active in reviewing state determinations. Even here there is a marked difference from the practice of the old Court in holding statutes unconstitutional. Under the older practice, measures like minimum-wage laws and price-control laws were held to be outside the pale of legislative authority. Under the modern practice, decisions of unconstitutionality tend to revolve about defects in procedure which can be remedied by the legislature. The Court is reminding both state and federal governments that they must turn square corners when they deal with sensitive areas of human liberty.

Consider the problem of internal security under the Constitution. The Court has held that the Smith Act is not unconstitutional, but that "advocacy" must be construed strictly, in a way that is close to the common-law concept of incitement.[9] The Court has held that loyalty oaths for state employees are not unconstitutional in themselves, but that they must provide certain requirements, notably a knowing state of mind.[10] When faced with the federal act virtually outlawing the Communist Party, the Court refrained from deciding the validity of the act for the reason that the record was tainted with the testimony of a discredited informer.[11] When confronted with legislative investigations of subversion, the Court has not uprooted the grand inquest of the nation, but has held that strict standards of relevance and precision must be followed when questions are put to a witness about his past associations.[12] When asked to rule on the validity of the denial of passports for security reasons, the Court found it possible to decline the invitation, interpreting stringently the legislative authority given to the State Department and concluding that sufficiently definite authority had not been delegated.[13] Similarly, a highly stringent reading of legislative authority enabled the Court to avoid basic constitutional questions regarding the discharge of government employees and employees in private defense plants.[14]

Unless one perceives the central theme running through all these decisions, one misses the significance of the Court's position in this troubled area of freedom and security. What are the characteristics of these decisions? In the first place the Court has followed a *via media*, recognizing that the problem has two faces. Second, the Court has put its emphasis on procedure, on due process in the primary meaning of the concept, for which the judiciary has special competence and responsibility. Third, the Court has given an opportunity to governmental agencies and the legislatures for solemn second thought—or, it may be, for first full and measured thought, as in the case of passport policy. Finally, the Court has kept the problems open-ended for itself, with room for movement later if necessary, as further experience, debate, and reflection may determine.

The Court has been exhibiting liberalism of a Lincolnian quality, not wholly satisfying the modern counterparts of either the abolitionists or the slaveholders. This is liberal statesmanship because it perceives the transcendent importance of fidelity to structure and process above attachment to the claims sponsored by the immediately contending parties.

Consider now the cases involving federal-state relations that gave most concern to the state chief justices. The Supreme Court has held that a man may not be denied admission to the bar simply because many years earlier, as a youth in the Depression period, he engaged in adventures with the Communist Party, adventures that he now finds repugnant, bringing as witnesses for his good faith, his minister, his teachers, neighbors, and fellow students.[15] The Court has held that a defendant in a criminal case must be provided a transcript for purposes of appeal if he is unable to afford the expense of paying for one, in all instances where such a transcript would be available to other, more fortunately situated, defendants.[16] The Court has held that a state attorney general may not question a lecturer at the state university about the content of his lectures, where he has denied advocating force and violence and where there is no evidence of such advocacy.[17] Can it be said that the foundations of the republic are really threatened by these decisions? Could it not rather be said that had these cases been decided otherwise there would have been cause for disquiet?

Of special concern to the state chief justices was the decision in *Commonwealth v. Nelson*,[18] affirming the Supreme Court of Pennsylvania, holding that a state antisubversive law applied to Communist leaders, where all the evidence was directed to advocacy of overthrow of the national government, is superseded by the federal Smith Act. The problem for the Court was to interpret the silence of Congress regarding the effect of the federal act on state legislation. In reaching its conclusion the Court was strongly affected by the fact that proper administration of an intelligence or counterintelligence program calls for unified interpretation and direction and prosecution. The conclusion is manifestly debatable; but no great constitutional issue is involved, and if the decision of the Pennsylvania and federal courts is as egregiously wrong as the highly vocal critics would insist, it is open to Congress to correct the error by a simple amendment to the Smith Act.

Indeed, a persuasive case can be made that in some of its decisions involving security and constitutional rights the Court has been excessively hospitable to the claims of the states. One group of decisions, concerning discharges of state employees for refusal to answer questions of a federal investigating committee, will be illustrative. In the *Slochower* case[19] the Court held unconstitutional a law providing for the automatic discharge of local employees who invoked the privilege against self-incrimination, as applied to a teacher who invoked the privilege before the House Un-American Activities Committee. Later it was held that a state board might validly discharge an employee for lack of fitness after inquiring into the circumstances of his invocation of the privilege.[20] These two holdings set the polar points within which variant cases would be decided. It was a very narrow spectrum, to be sure.

Then a case arose in California testing which of the poles had the stronger magnetic force. A temporary employee who claimed his constitutional privilege before the House Committee was summarily discharged under a state law requiring employees to testify before such committees and providing for dismissal upon refusal to answer questions on any ground whatsoever. How should the case have been decided? If *Slochower* rested on the ground that due process requires individualized treatment by the employing agency in order to take account of the witness' motives, the relevance of the questions, and similar factors bearing on his fitness, then the California case, involving as it did a summary discharge, should have been decided in favor of the employee. If *Slochower* rested on the ground that the state was there drawing an improper statutory inference of guilt from the assertion of the privilege, then the California case was perhaps distinguishable, since the statute did not single out the claim of self-incrimination as ground for discharge (though in fact this was the employee's ground for refusal to answer questions of the House Committee). The Court, in a closely divided decision, took the latter position, sustaining the discharge.[21] The issue, characteristically, is one of procedure rather than of basic sovereign rights. It may be regretted that the Court did not require more individualized treatment. In an age increasingly defaced by anonymity and mass media, mass politics and mass information, factories with so many "hands," armies with so many "bodies," it is all the more vital that the reality of human personality be respected where it is still feasible to do so. Procedural due process is a constitutional mandate that might well have compelled the state to take a closer individual look before discharging persons who asserted a constitutional testimonial privilege before a federal agency.

On the side of its own jurisdiction and procedure, the record of the Court is not wholly reassuring. The Court is now confronted with almost two thousand cases a year, of which about two hundred are selected for decision on the merits. Members of the Court have repeatedly importuned the bar to refrain from filing petitions in cases that are clearly not worthy of Supreme Court review. At best, such admonitions are likely to be futile. But, in any event, they are hardly likely to meet with success when lawyers observe the kind of cases that on occasion the Court is prepared to review. This mounting docket of cases looms as a serious barrier to the true mission of the Supreme Court: to clarify, expound, and develop the law in its most significant national aspects, and not to act as a mere further appellate court for the correction of possible error. The Court itself has adopted expedients to cope with its burden of cases: a number of cases are allotted even less time for oral argument than the normal hour to a side; and a growing number of cases are decided without a full opinion, some of them without the benefit of full briefs and argument. These expedients, with respect, appear to be a movement in the wrong direction, in the direction, that is, away from the fullest possible consideration, consultation, reflection, and exposition.

A very different remedy has been suggested by Dean Griswold: the withdrawal of certain types of cases from the statutory jurisdiction of the Supreme Court and the vesting of them in a specialized court of last resort; tax cases would be the specific category most favored for such treatment.[22] Before consideration is given to proposals of this sort, which have thoughtful reasons behind them, but which raise qualms about a supreme tribunal of specialists, I would hope that the Court will employ a measure of self-help by adopting stricter, more Brandeisian standards in the granting of review, thereby reducing the number of oral arguments and the volume of opinion writing, gaining additional time for study and deliberation, and perhaps discouraging counsel from filing a certain number of unmeritorious petitions for review. The Court is entitled to those conditions of work which will minimize the risk of the hasty, the flimsy, and the untested. Judging is a high art, and the judge, like the artist, must feel that the shoddy is an offense against his medium, as a lie is a sin against language.

When we come to examine this final aspect of the Court's performance—its craftsmanship—our judgment is likely to be mixed. Let me illustrate. In recounting certain of the cases that were criticized by the state chief justices, I was guilty of the kind of oversimplification that has sometimes marked the opinions themselves. On the subject of admission to the bar, for example, there were two companion cases, one from New Mexico and one from California, which were superficially similar and which reached similar results, but which from the standpoint of legal analysis presented very different problems. The New Mexico case involved the set of facts that I have previously described, the rejection of an applicant for admission to the bar on the ground of earlier Communist activities. But the California case involved an applicant who was not as candid, who in fact refused to answer questions regarding his Communist affiliations.[23] This line of questioning was relevant, or so it would seem the state authorities might have regarded it, to determine the applicant's veracity and the validity of his self-serving statements regarding his good character and attachment to the principles of the Constitution. And yet the Court reversed the action of the California tribunals, holding that the refusal to answer was not adequate evidence on the score of good moral character, the standard that the state law required the applicant to satisfy affirmatively for admission to the bar.

There was similarly a pair of cases involving legislative investigations, one under the House Un-American Activities Committee's jurisdiction and the other under the authority of the legislature of New Hampshire, which had delegated jurisdiction to the state Attorney General.[24] The federal case required for decision only a holding that the witness had not been adequately informed of the subject under investigation, so that he could judge the relevance of the questions he was asked. The New Hampshire case was decided with an opinion that questioned whether the legislature of New Hampshire had actually authorized the line of questioning the Attorney General had pursued. But this issue had been resolved in favor of the state by the highest court of the state and hardly seemed to present a federal question. A concurring opinion by Mr. Justice Frankfurter took the ground, which seems inescapable as a necessary support for the decision, that the interrogation of the witness was too great an intrusion into the area of intellectual freedom, particularly since there had been no evidence that he was engaging in any call to action or that he was fomenting disobedience to law.

Another pair of cases concerned the right of an indigent criminal defendant to be furnished a trial transcript for purposes of appeal.[25] The Court made new and salutary law in holding that this was a requirement of equal protection of the laws. But did it necessarily follow that this new constitutional principle must be applied to cases long since closed, where the trial judge had found that justice would not be promoted by such an appeal, with the result that convicted persons serving their sentences must be allowed to seek their release on habeas corpus if the state did not recognize years ago this newly declared right? The answer involves considerations, not only of principle but also of practical administration, that seem to call at least for some further delineation; but the problem was disposed of summarily on the authority of the earlier decision.

The conflict between freedom of speech and compelled disclosure provides another illustration. A Los Angeles ordinance required all handbills to contain the names of the printer and the sponsor of the document. Is such a requirement consistent with the guarantee of freedom of speech and press? Some guidelines had been furnished by precedents. The Court had held that the distribution of political leaflets could not be forbidden or subjected to a licensing authority;[26] and, on the issue of compelled disclosure, it had held that membership lists of the N.A.A.C.P. could not be subpoenaed by state authorities in connection with a contest over the Association's doing of business in the state.[27] On the other hand, the Court had sustained laws requiring publication of the names of the editors and owners of newspapers using second-class mailing privileges,[28] and had upheld the detailed requirements of disclosure imposed on lobbying organizations;[29] moreover, most states have laws prohibiting the distribution of anonymous publications with reference to political candidates. All of these precedents obviously entailed a weighing of the public value served by disclosure against its repressive effect on free expression. In the Los Angeles case the public purpose was said to be the identification of those responsible for defamatory, fraudulent, or otherwise actionable material. A majority of the Court decided that the interest in the dissemination of unpopular ideas was paramount to any such generalized protective purpose of the law.[30] But the bearing of the other precedents, though stressed in the dissenting opinion, was not discussed by the majority. Nor was any consideration given in the opinion to a philosophy of free speech which would regard a modicum of identification of the source as an aid to, not an impairment of, a free market in ideas. If such is a rational, though debatable, philosophy, is a community precluded from acting upon it as a permissible balance between the interest of purveyors of handbills and that of the reading public? Whatever one's ultimate answer, it is disappointing that the question was not treated as a profoundly genuine one.

The polarization, it must be added, has not been all in one direction. Again in the field of compulsory disclosure, more particularly as it concerns legislative investigations, there has been a hardening of positions on both sides: on the part of one group, an absolutist protection from inquiry into memberships and associations is demanded; on the part of the other, a countervailing "balancing" of the public interest, which it quite regularly finds adequate to warrant the questioning. The "balancing" figure, against which Justice Black has repeatedly protested, is unfortunate if it assumes a choice between two polarities; if a metaphor is wanted, a spectrum of tones would be more promising of closer analysis and reconciliation. Questions directed to Communist Party membership aside, requirements might be laid down of independent evidence linking the witness or the organization to punishable activity as a condition of inquiry into political associations, or alternatively, that the evidence be taken in executive session and names be undisclosed in published reports.

These examples suggest that in some instances the Court may be too ready to carry a sound principle beyond the point where it collides with a sound principle rubbing against it from the other direction—those clashes of right with right, "between whose endless jar justice resides." Or, to pass from the Bard to Mr. Justice Holmes, "All rights tend to declare themselves absolute to their logical extreme. Yet all in fact are limited by the neighborhood of principles of policy which are other than those on which the particular right is founded, and which become strong enough to hold their own when a certain point is reached."[31]

The thrust of the criticism by the state chief justices seems to me, in short, to have been misdirected. There has been no real invasion of state authority; on the contrary, there has been growing acceptance of state legislation in the matters that really count for the states. What the Court has done is to insist on procedural observances by both federal and state agencies, and on the standards of fair play which are implicit in the concept of due process of law. It is not particularly useful to count the number of times the Court has reversed lower federal courts or state courts. What is more important is to understand the basis for such reversals. In this light it will be seen that the Court is concerned with method, procedures, and similar elements that go to the way in which legal authority is exercised against the individual, leaving it to the state or federal government to cure the defect by more careful procedures, or perchance, on taking a longer second look, to reconsider the basic policy and objectives of its program.

What gives concern is not, then, what seems to have chiefly troubled the state chief justices. It is rather a tendency to make broad principles do service for specific problems that call for differentiation, a tendency toward overbroadness that is not an augury of enduring work and that misses the opportunity to use the litigation process for the refinement and adaptation of principle to meet the variety of concrete issues as they are presented in a lawsuit. Mr. Justice Holmes said, in another of his shock-the-multitude moods: "I hate justice." What he meant, he went on to say, was that when people began talking about justice they were likely to be trying to escape from law. Holmes's witticism is a caution against judging the judges simply in terms of end results. The law of the future is likely to be the law that earns its perdurance by solidity and strength of workmanship no less than by the appeal its results make to our ethical sense. For, as I have tried to show in the essay on Brandeis, the quality of the judge's performance is at bottom an ethical responsibility, and this element cannot be separated in the end from the ethical appeal made by a judicial decision.

Legal method, like scientific method, entails ethical decisions along the way, which are not always recognized as such. Our law, like science, proceeds from specific instances to tentative generalizations, which are in turn tested, refined, and recast. The process involves at least two deep-seated problems that are commonly left obscure. There is, in the first place, the perpetually baffling problem of inductive logic, which depends on a selection of "similarities" and "differences," a selection that is necessarily purposive. In the second place, there is the question how much of the framework of the subject ought to be re-examined, how regressive should be the reconsideration of premises, in resolving a troublesome series of instances—a determination that again involves a judgment of values—of fidelity to the past, of greater simplicity and predictability and coherence, of conservation of human energy.[32] These problems, as I have said, are implicit in science as in law. When it is remembered that, in addition, the end of the legal process is itself prescriptive, the ethical elements in the process are seen to be complex and pervasive.

We do not enjoy a superabundance of institutions engaged in the rational pursuit of truth and right. As a law teacher, I think of the universities and the courts. Students and judges are trained to turn up their collars against windy sloganeering, no matter from which direction it is blown. Can any discipline be more valuable today than one that teaches us to look through the great antinomies that present themselves like gladiators for our favors—individualism and collectivism, liberty and authority, secularism and clericalism—to look through them in order to discover the precise issue in controversy, the precise consequences of one decision or another, and the possibility of an accommodation by deflating the isms and narrowing the schisms? This is the task, and at its best, the accomplishment of the law, and particularly of the judges in constitutional law. A judge writing for the popular anthologies could readily compose an essay on the side of liberty of speech or on the side of public order; but a judge devoted to his mission will resist the temptation. When he exposes the factors that trouble the judgment, strives for as particularistic a decision as he can make, and gives a reasoned elaboration, he is providing a lesson in the rational solution of human conflicts that is too precious to be jeopardized through disrespect.

It is too precious, also, to be at the hazard of internal pressures from the Court's work load that interfere with the essential processes of reflection, consultation, collective criticism, and careful exposition. If the Court saw fit to adjust its procedures to these ends, the bar and the public ought to accept the practices with understanding, even though this might involve the granting of fewer petitions for review and some longer waits for decisions.

The bar has a threefold opportunity to serve the best interests of the Court: by adjusting itself to the procedures called for by the Court's exceptional jurisdiction and unique responsibilities; by providing advocacy, in briefs and oral argument, as well-focused and scholarly as might have been provided by a more distinct Supreme Court bar, such as existed at the beginning; and by interpreting the Court fairly and informatively to the general public. The law schools, on their part, have been slow to assume a responsibility for providing the reliable and disinterested interpretation of Court decisions which should be part of the process of popular education. Local law schools and the local press could find ways to co-operate usefully in this enterprise.

One can imagine the Court asking simply, in the

words of Othello, "Nothing extenuate, nor set down aught in malice." Or, with Hamlet, "Report us and our cause aright to the unsatisfied." But when one remembers that these were the words of tragic heroes in their dying moments, as they were about to succumb to wounds self-inflicted or self-invited, one hesitates over the literary parallels. In the Court's crisis salvation will come, as in other secular crises, partly from within and partly from without.

★

# SELECTED READINGS


HISTORY

Warren, Charles. *The Supreme Court in United States History*. 2 vols. Boston: Little, Brown & Co. Rev. ed., 1926.

Swisher, Carl B. *American Constitutional Development*. Boston: Houghton Mifflin Co., 1943.

Hurst, James Willard. *Law and the Conditions of Freedom in the Nineteenth-Century United States*. Madison: University of Wisconsin Press, 1956.

McCloskey, Robert G. *The American Supreme Court*. Chicago: University of Chicago Press, 1960.

THE ROLE OF JUDICIAL REVIEW

Sutherland, Arthur E., ed. *Government Under Law*. Cambridge, Mass.: Harvard University Press, 1956.

Frankfurter, Felix. *Of Law and Men*. New York: Harcourt, Brace & Co., 1956.

Hand, Learned. *The Bill of Rights*. Cambridge, Mass.: Harvard University Press, 1958.

Jackson, Robert H. *The Supreme Court in the American*

*System of Government*. Cambridge, Mass.: Harvard University Press, 1955.

Black, Charles L., Jr. *The People and the Court: Judicial Review in a Democracy*. New York: Macmillan Co., 1960.

Wechsler, Herbert. *Principles, Politics, and Fundamental Law*. Cambridge, Mass.: Harvard University Press, 1961.

Cahn, Edmond N., ed. *Supreme Court and Supreme Law*. Bloomington: Indiana University Press, 1954.

THE FEDERAL SYSTEM

Macmahon, Arthur W. *Federalism Mature and Emergent*. New York: Doubleday & Co., 1955.

Bowie, Robert R., and Friedrich, Carl J., eds. *Studies in Federalism*. Boston: Little, Brown & Co., 1954.

Powell, Thomas Reed. *Vagaries and Varieties in Constitutional Interpretation*. New York: Columbia University Press, 1956.

CIVIL LIBERTIES

Chafee, Zechariah, Jr. *Free Speech in the United States*. Cambridge, Mass.: Harvard University Press, 1941.

Gellhorn, Walter. *American Rights*. New York: Macmillan Co., 1960.

Greenberg, Jack. *Race Relations and American Law*. New York: Columbia University Press, 1959.

Meiklejohn, Alexander. *Political Freedom: The Constitutional Powers of the People*. New York: Harper and Brothers, 1960.

Griswold, Erwin N. *The Fifth Amendment Today*. Cambridge, Mass.: Harvard University Press, 1955.

Konvitz, Milton R. *Bill of Rights Reader*. Ithaca: Cornell University Press, 1954.

COUNSEL AND THE COURT

Jackson, Robert H. *The Struggle for Judicial Supremacy*. New York: Alfred A. Knopf, 1941.

Twiss, Benjamin R., *Lawyers and the Constitution*. Princeton: Princeton University Press, 1942.

Stern, Robert L., and Gressman, Eugene. *Supreme Court Practice*. Washington: Bureau of National Affairs, 2nd ed., 1954.

DATE MAR 31 1965

EMPLOYEE NUMBER 3-06065

# NON-NEGOTIABLE

STATEMENT OF EARNINGS AND DEDUCTIONS

165899

| | | | | | |
|---|---|---|---|---|---|
| 120.00 | | | | 2.80 | |
| GROSS EARNINGS | PERQUISITE | MEDICAL PLAN | S. I. A. | RETIREMENT CONTRIBUTION | INS. - BONDS ETC. |
| | 16.80 | 3.99 | 4.35 | | 92.06 |
| ASSIGNMENT | FED. TAX | STATE TAX | F.I.C.A. | | NET |

## OREGON STATE SYSTEM OF HIGHER EDUCATION

### COMPTROLLER'S OFFICE — CORVALLIS, OREGON

OREGON STATE UNIVERSITY, CORVALLIS
PORTLAND STATE COLLEGE, PORTLAND
OREGON COLLEGE OF EDUCATION, MONMOUTH
EASTERN OREGON COLLEGE, LA GRANDE
SOUTHERN OREGON COLLEGE, ASHLAND

UNIVERSITY OF OREGON, EUGENE
UNIVERSITY OF OREGON MEDICAL SCHOOL, PORTLAND
UNIVERSITY OF OREGON DENTAL SCHOOL, PORTLAND
GENERAL EXTENSION DIVISION, PORTLAND, CORVALLIS, EUGENE
OREGON TECHNICAL INSTITUTE, KLAMATH FALLS
DIVISION OF CONTINUING EDUCATION

Ⓟ v

MEMBERS OF THE COURT

Dunham, Allison, and Kurland, Philip B., eds. *Mr. Justice.* Chicago: University of Chicago Press, 1956. (Essays by nine authors on Marshall, Taney, Bradley, Holmes, Brandeis, Sutherland, Stone, Hughes, and Rutledge.)

Frankfurter, Felix. *Mr. Justice Holmes and the Supreme Court.* Cambridge, Mass.: Harvard University Press, 1961.

Frankfurter, Felix, ed. *Mr. Justice Brandeis.* New Haven: Yale University Press, 1932.

Konefsky, Samuel J. *The Legacy of Holmes and Brandeis.* New York: Macmillan Co., 1956.

Lerner, Max. *The Mind and Faith of Justice Holmes.* Boston: Little, Brown & Co., 1943.

Mason, Alpheus T. *Brandeis: A Free Man's Life.* New York: Viking Press, 1946.

Bickel, Alexander M. *The Unpublished Opinions of Mr. Justice Brandeis.* Cambridge, Mass.: Harvard University Press, 1957.

Mason, Alpheus T. *Harlan Fisk Stone: Pillar of the Law.* New York: Viking Press, 1956.

Konefsky, Samuel J. *The Constitutional World of Mr. Justice Frankfurter.* New York: Macmillan Co., 1949.

Thomas, Helen S. *Felix Frankfurter: Scholar on the Bench.* Baltimore: Johns Hopkins Press, 1960.

Frank, John P. *Mr. Justice Black: The Man and His Opinions.* New York: Alfred A. Knopf, 1949.

Countryman, Vern. *Douglas of the Supreme Court: A Selection of His Opinions.* New York: Doubleday & Co., 1959.

Westin, Alan F., ed. *The Supreme Court: Views from Inside.* New York: W. W. Norton & Co., 1961.

## NOTES

I. THE BUSINESS OF THE COURT

1. For the part played by Chief Justice Hughes in this development, and for an illuminating account of the administrative side of the Court, see McElwain, "The Business of the Supreme Court as Conducted by Chief Justice Hughes," 63 *Harv. L. Rev.* 5 (1949), with a Foreword by Mr. Justice Frankfurter.

2. A *locus classicus* for this principle and its corollaries is the concurring opinion of Brandeis, J., in Ashwander v. TVA, 297 U.S. 288, 341 (1936); see also Rutledge, J., in Rescue Army v. Municipal Court, 331 U.S. 549 (1947).

3. Dred Scott v. Sandford, 19 How. 393 (1857).

4. Pollock v. Farmers Loan & Trust Co., 157 U.S. 429, 158 U.S. 601 (1895).

5. Hughes, *The Supreme Court of the United States* (1928), 50-54. The third of the ill-starred triad was Hepburn v. Griswold, 8 Wall. 603 (1870), overruled in Legal Tender Cases, 12 Wall. 457 (1871).

6. 16 Pet. 1 (1842).

7. Erie RR. v. Tompkins, 304 U.S. 64 (1938).

8. Art. I, Sec. 8: "The Congress shall have Power . . . to regulate Commerce with Foreign Nations, and among the several States, and with the Indian Tribes."

9. McCulloch v. Maryland, 4 Wheat. 316, at p. 413 (1819).

10. Missouri v. Holland, 252 U.S. 416, 433 (1920).

11. Gompers v. U.S., 233 U.S. 604, 610 (1914).

12. Home Bldg. & Loan Assn. v. Blaisdell, 290 U.S. 398, 442-43 (1943).

13. Carter v. Carter Coal Co., 298 U.S. 238 (1936) (Cardozo, Brandeis, and Stone, JJ., dissenting); cf. Coronado Coal Co. v. United Mine Workers, 268 U.S. 295 (1925) (conspiracy under antitrust laws). For a particularly vigorous dissent by Hughes, C. J., from a restrictive commerce-clause decision see Railroad Retirement Bd. v. Alton RR., 295 U.S. 330, 374 (1935).

14. A vivid account of the Court's performance before and after the Court plan is contained in Mr. Justice (then Attorney General) Jackson's book, *The Struggle for Judicial Supremacy* (1941). The current scope of national power under the commerce clause is perhaps sufficiently revealed by Wickard v. Filburn, 317 U.S. 111 (1942) (sustaining acreage quotas for wheat, including wheat consumed on the farm).

15. Compare Missouri Pac. RR. v. Norwood, 283 U.S. 249 (1931), with Southern Pac. Co. v. Arizona, 325 U.S. 761 (1945).

16. In the *Southern Pacific* case (see above, n. 15) the printed record extends to 4,088 pages.

17. Compare H. P. Hood & Sons v. DuMond, 336 U.S. 525 (1949), with Milk Board v. Eisenberg Co., 306 U.S. 346 (1939); and Buck v. Kuykendall, 267 U.S. 307 (1925), with Robertson v. California, 328 U.S. 440 (1946).

18. The act was passed over the veto and was sustained in Clark Distilling Co. v. Western Md. Ry., 242 U.S. 311 (1917).

19. United States v. South-Eastern Underwriters Assn., 322 U.S. 533 (1944).

20. The act was sustained in Prudential Ins. Co. v. Benjamin, 328 U.S. 408 (1946).

21. Steward Machine Co. v. Davis, 301 U.S. 548 (1937).

22. Testa v. Katt, 330 U.S. 386 (1947) (Price Control Act).

23. Anderson v. Dunn, 6 Wheat. 204, 226 (1821).

24. Amend. I: "Congress shall make no law respecting an

establishment of religion, or prohibiting the free exercise thereof; or abridging the freedom of speech, or of the press; or the right of the people peaceably to assemble and to petition the Government for a redress of grievances."

Amend. V: "No person shall be . . . deprived of life, liberty, or property, without due process of law."

Amend. XIV: ". . . nor shall any State deprive any person of life, liberty, or property, without due process of law."

25. See Black, J., in Bridges v. California, 314 U.S. 252, 263 (1941).

26. See Cardozo, J., in Palko v. Connecticut, 302 U.S. 319, 326-27 (1937).

27. See Stone, J., in United States v. Carolene Products Co., 304 U.S. 144, 152, n. 4 (1938).

28. Meiklejohn, *Free Speech* (1948), 32.

29. On the history and practice see John P. Frank, "The Appointment of Supreme Court Justices: Prestige, Principles and Politics," 1941 *Wis. L. Rev.* 172, 343, 461.

30. Burnet v. Coronado Oil & Gas Co., 285 U.S. 393, 406-08 (1932) (dissenting). The opinion of Brandeis, J., collects the decisions that overruled precedents; see also the valuable article by Sharp, "Movement in Supreme Court Adjudication—A Study of Modified and Overruled Decisions," 46 *Harv. L. Rev.* 361, 593, 795 (1933). Mr. Justice Douglas has put in extreme terms the responsibility for judicial re-examination: Douglas, "Stare Decisis," 49 *Col. L. Rev.* 735 (1949) (containing a table of 30 overruling cases in the period 1937-49).

31. Passenger Cases, 7 How. 282, 470 (1849).

II. CONCORD AND DISCORD

1. Fairman, *Mr. Justice Miller and the Supreme Court* (1939), 232.

2. Whitehead, *Essays in Science and Philosophy* (1947), 130.

3. Address of Chief Justice Hughes, 13 *Proc. Am. L. Inst.* 61, 64 (1936): "How amazing it is that, in the midst of controversies on every conceivable subject, one should expect unanimity of opinion upon difficult legal questions! In the highest ranges of thought, in theology, philosophy and science, we find differences of view on the part of the most distinguished experts—theologians, philosophers and scien-

tists. The history of scholarship is a record of disagreements. And when we deal with questions relating to principles of law and their application, we do not suddenly rise into a stratosphere of icy certainty."

4. West Virginia State Board of Education v. Barnette, 319 U.S. 624 (1943). The earlier cases are Leoles v. Lander, 302 U.S. 656 (1937); Hering v. State Board of Education, 303 U.S. 624 (1938).

5. Grovey v. Townsend, 295 U.S. 45 (1935); Smith v. Allwright, 321 U.S. 649 (1944).

6. Shelley v. Kraemer, 334 U.S. 1 (1948). The earlier case is Corrigan v. Buckley, 271 U.S. 323 (1926).

7. Commonwealth v. Davis, 162 Mass. 510, 511 (1895). Cf. Hague v. C.I.O., 307 U.S. 496 (1939).

8. United Public Workers v. Mitchell, 330 U.S. 75 (1947), quoting (at p. 99, n. 34) Holmes's remark in McAuliffe v. New Bedford, 155 Mass. 216, 220 (1891).

9. Kovacs v. Cooper, 336 U.S. 77, 95 (1949) (concurring).

10. Cf. Hocking, *Freedom of the Press* (1947), 60-61: "The right of freedom is based on the value of freedom but is not identical with that value. . . . Why is one not free to abandon his freedom; why may he not sell himself into slavery? Because, quite apart from his inclination, he has a duty to live as a man and assume the burden of self-guidance. He owes this to his own dignity; he owes it also to the common concern that human dignity shall be upheld." Ibid. at 96-97: "If a man is burdened with an idea, he not only desires to express it; he ought to express it. . . . It is the duty of the scientist or the discoverer to his result, of Confucius to his teaching, of Socrates to his oracle. It is the duty of every man to his belief. It is not limited to special persons and special occasions; it has a certain totality. . . . In any case, one's relation to what he himself *sees* constitutes for him a major obligation, and the freedom of expression here merges with freedom of conscience."

11. Cf. the well-known statement of Stone, J., in United States v. Carolene Products Co., 304 U.S. 144, 152, n. 4 (1938):

"It is unnecessary to consider now whether legislation which restricts those political processes which can ordinarily be expected to bring about repeal of undesirable legislation, is to be subjected to more exacting judicial scrutiny under the general prohibitions of the Fourteenth Amendment than are most other types of legislation. . . .

"Nor need we enquire whether similar considerations enter into the review of statutes directed at particular religious . . . or national . . . or racial minorities . . .: whether prejudice against discrete and insular minorities may be a special condition, which tends seriously to curtail the operation of those political processes ordinarily to be relied upon to protect minorities, and which may call for a correspondingly more searching judicial inquiry. Compare McCulloch v. Maryland, 4 Wheat. 316, 428; South Carolina v. Barnwell Bros., 303 U.S. 177, 184, n. 2, and cases cited."

When we move from legislative clogs on the political processes themselves, in the large sense, to the kind of legislation dealt with at the end of the final paragraph, there is the difficulty of distinguishing between minorities of the kind specified and some economic minority interests, so far as concerns the operation of representative government through majority rule. The cases last cited in the paragraph are distinctive, since they are instances of local economic interests working against the outsider, raising problems of federalism.

12. See Charles Warren, "The New 'Liberty' under the Fourteenth Amendment," 39 *Harv. L. Rev.* 431 (1926).

13. L. Hand, "Chief Justice Stone's Conception of the Judicial Function," 46 *Col. L. Rev.* 696, 698 (1946).

14. *Discourses on Davila* (1789-90), quoted in Coker, *Democracy, Liberty, and Property* (1947), 466.

15. "A Defence of the Constitutions of Government of the United States of America," in J. Adams, *Works* (C. F. Adams, ed., 1851), VI, 9.

16. *Construction Construed, and Constitutions Vindicated* (1820), quoted in Coker, op. cit., at 495-96.

17. *Journal of Debates and Proceedings in the Convention of Delegates Chosen to Revise the Constitution of Massachusetts, 1820* (1853), 312.

18. Letter to Moss Kent, in *Memoirs and Letters of James Kent* (1898), 218.

19. *The Law of Love and Love as Law* (1868), 182-83, quoted in Gabriel, *The Course of American Democratic Thought* (1940), 149.

20. *Shelburne Essays*, 9th Series (1915), 136 (italics in original). For the reference I am indebted to Professor Merle

Curti of the University of Wisconsin. Cf. also Babbitt, *Democracy and Leadership* (1924), 307-08.

21. Lincoln Federal Labor Union v. Northwestern Iron & Metal Co., 335 U.S. 525 (1949).

22. Hocking, *Freedom of the Press*, p. 56.

23. Reprinted in Wolfe, *Leveller Manifestoes of the Puritan Revolution* (1944), 400, 409.

24. Reprinted in Edman, *Fountainheads of Freedom* (1941), 320, 324-25.

25. Murdock v. Pennsylvania, 319 U.S. 105 (1943) (Roberts, Reed, Frankfurter, and Jackson, JJ., dissenting); Martin v. Struthers, 319 U.S. 141 (1943) (Roberts, Reed, Frankfurter, and Jackson, JJ., dissenting; Douglas, Murphy, and Rutledge, JJ., concurring specially); Saia v. New York, 334 U.S. 558 (1948) (Reed, Frankfurter, Jackson, Burton, JJ., dissenting); cf. Kovacs v. Cooper (above, n. 9) (Black, Douglas, Murphy, and Rutledge, JJ., dissenting; Frankfurter and Jackson, JJ., concurring specially).

26. *In re* Summers, 325 U.S. 561 (1945) (Black, Douglas, Murphy, and Rutledge, JJ., dissenting).

27. Harris v. United States, 331 U.S. 145 (1947) (upholding seizure, without a search warrant, of unlawfully possessed draft cards after intensive search of premises pursuant to warrant of arrest for unrelated offense; Frankfurter, Murphy, Jackson, and Rutledge, JJ., dissenting); Johnson v. United States, 333 U.S. 10 (1948) (invalidating search and seizure of opium and smoking apparatus in living quarters, without warrant of arrest or of search; Vinson, C. J., Black, Reed, and Burton, JJ., dissenting); Trupiano v. United States, 334 U.S. 699 (1948) (invalidating seizure of contraband property, where arrest was lawful but no search warrant was obtained and failure not justified by emergency; Vinson, C. J., Black, Reed, and Burton, JJ., dissenting). Compare Abel v. U.S., 362 U.S. 217 (1960); Frank v. Maryland, 359 U.S. 360 (1959).

28. Commonwealth v. Peaslee, 177 Mass. 267, 272 (1901); cf. also Swift & Co. v. United States, 196 U.S. 375, 396 (1905); Hyde v. United States, 225 U.S. 347, 387, 388 (1912) (dissenting).

29. Bridges v. California, 314 U.S. 252 (1941) (Stone, C. J., Roberts, Frankfurter, and Byrnes, JJ., dissenting).

30. United Public Workers v. Mitchell (above, n. 8) (Black,

Douglas, and Rutledge, JJ., dissenting; Frankfurter, J., concurring specially; Murphy and Jackson, JJ., not participating).

31. McNabb v. United States, 318 U.S. 332 (1943).

32. Townsend v. Burke, 334 U.S. 736, 738 (1948).

33. Fisher v. United States, 328 U.S. 463 (1946).

34. Uveges v. Pennsylvania, 335 U.S. 437, 449-50 (1948) (dissenting).

35. Pinkerton v. United States, 328 U.S. 640 (1946); Kotteakos v. United States, 328 U.S. 750 (1946); see Krulewitch v. United States, 336 U.S. 440 (1949). Compare Callanan v. United States, 364 U.S. 587 (1961).

36. Adamson v. California, 332 U.S. 46, 68-123 (1947) (dissenting).

37. Ibid. at 69-70, 77-78, 90, 91. See also the concurring opinion in International Shoe Co. v. Washington, 326 U.S. 310, 322 (1945).

38. Connecticut Gen. Life Ins. Co. v. Johnson, 303 U.S. 77, 83 (1938) (dissenting).

39. 307 U.S. 496, 500 (1939).

40. 314 U.S. at 280.

41. 332 U.S. at 71.

42. Frank, Book Review, 24 *Ind. L. J.* 139, 144, n. 10 (1948).

43. "Science and Morals" (1886), in *Evolution and Ethics, and Other Essays* (1897), 128.

44. In sequence the later cases are Rochin v. California, 342 U.S. 165 (1952); Elkins v. U.S., 364 U.S. 206 (1960) (Frankfurter, Clark, Harlan, and Whittaker, J.J. dissenting); Mapp v. Ohio, decided June 19, 1961 (Harlan, Frankfurter, and Whittaker, J.J. dissenting).

45. Johnson v. Zerbst, 304 U.S. 458 (1938).

46. Betts v. Brady, 316 U.S. 455 (1942); Bute v. Illinois, 333 U.S. 640 (1948). The thesis that the workings of federalism would be promoted, not exacerbated, by enforcing the right to counsel against the states in all criminal cases is ably presented in J. R. Green, "The Bill of Rights, the Fourteenth Amendment and the Supreme Court," 46 *Mich. L. Rev.* 869 (1948).

47. H. A. L. Fisher, *Maitland* (1910), 67.

48. United States v. South-Eastern Underwriters Assn.,

322 U.S. 533 (1944) (departing from precedent; Stone, C. J., Frankfurter and Jackson, JJ., dissenting; Roberts and Reed, JJ., not participating).

49. Helvering v. Griffiths, 318 U.S. 371 (1943) (adhering to precedent; Douglas, Black, and Murphy, JJ., dissenting; Rutledge, J., not participating).

50. Girouard v. United States, 328 U.S. 61 (1946) (departing from precedent; Stone, C. J., Reed and Frankfurter, JJ., dissenting; Jackson, J., not participating).

51. Cleveland v. United States, 329 U.S. 14 (1946) (adhering to precedent; Black, Murphy, and Jackson, JJ., dissenting; Rutledge, J., concurring specially).

52. 318 U.S. at 408.

53. Helvering v. Griffiths (above, n. 49), at 403-04; United States v. California, 332 U.S. 19, 45-46 (1947) (dissent); Commisioner v. Estate of Church, 335 U.S. 632, 685, n. 14 (1949) (dissent).

54. Helvering v. Gerhardt, 304 U.S. 405 (1938).

55. Message from the President, April 25, 1938, 83 *Cong. Rec.* 5683.

56. "Memorandum in Reply to Petition for Rehearing" in Helvering v. Gerhardt (above, n. 54), at 16-18.

57. 53 Stat. 575.

58. L. Hand, "Thomas Walter Swan," 57 *Yale L. J.* 167, 172 (1947).

III. STANDARDS FOR CIVIL LIBERTIES

1. Kunz v. People of State of New York, 340 U.S. 290, 299 (1951).

2. Meyer v. Nebraska, 262 U.S. 390 (1923); Pierce v. Society of Sisters, 268 U.S. 510 (1925).

3. Gitlow v. New York, 268 U.S. 652 (1925).

4. Schneider v. State (Town of Irvington), 308 U.S. 147 (1939); Cantwell v. Connecticut, 310 U.S. 296 (1940).

5. Minersville School District v. Gobitis, 310 U.S. 586 (1940); West Virginia State Board of Education v. Barnette, 319 U.S. 624 (1943).

6. E.g., Near v. Minnesota, 283 U.S. 697 (1931); Herndon v. Lowry, 301 U.S. 242 (1937).

7. De Jonge v. Oregon, 299 U.S. 353 (1937); Hague v. C.I.O., 307 U.S. 496 (1939).

8. See above, n. 5.

9. Everson v. Board of Education, 330 U.S. 1 (1947); cf. Illinois *ex rel.* McCollum v. Board of Education, 333 U.S. 203, 210, 233 (1948). See, generally, the symposium on "Religion and the State," 14 *Law & Contemp. Prob.* 1 (1949).

10. Cf. Bridges v. California, 314 U.S. 252 (1941); Pennekamp v. Florida, 328 U.S. 331 (1946).

11. United States v. Classic, 313 U.S. 299 (1941); United States v. Saylor, 322 U.S. 385 (1944).

12. See Brandeis, J., concurring, in Whitney v. California, 274 U.S. 357, 379-80, (1927).

13. Colegrove v. Green, 328 U.S. 549 (1946) (Congressional districts); South v. Peters, 339 U.S. 276 (1950) (county unit system); cf. McDougall v. Green, 335 U.S. 281 (1948) (distribution of signers of nominating petition).

14. 4 Wheat. 316, 401 (1819).

15. Children's Hospital v. Adkins, 284 Fed. 613, 622 (D.C. Cir. 1922), quoted in Jackson, *The Struggle for Judicial Supremacy* (1941), 74.

16. Valentine v. Chrestensen, 316 U.S. 52 (1942).

17. Lovell v. City of Griffin, 303 U.S. 444 (1938).

18. Purity Extract & Tonic Co. v. Lynch, 226 U.S. 192 (1912) (near-beer).

19. Winters v. New York, 333 U.S. 507 (1948) (crime magazines).

20. See Electric Bond & Share Co. v. SEC, 303 U.S. 419, 437-38 (1938).

21. Thomas v. Collins, 323 U.S. 516 (1945).

22. Great Atlantic & Pacific Tea Co. v. Grosjean, 301 U.S. 412 (1937).

23. Grosjean v. American Press Co., 297 U.S. 233 (1936).

24. E.g., Federal Trade Commission v. Standard Education Society, 302 U.S. 112 (1937); Gray v. Powell, 314 U.S. 402 (1941); cf. Phillips v. Comm'r, 283 U.S. 589 (1931); Brandeis, J., concurring, in St. Joseph Stock Yards Co. v. United States, 298 U.S. 38, 77 (1936) ("The second distinction is between the right to liberty of person and other constitutional rights").

25. E.g., Ng Fung Ho v. White, 259 U.S. 276 (1922); Bridges v. Wixon, 326 U.S. 135 (1945).

26. United States v. Sullivan, 332 U.S. 689 (1948).

27. Hannegan v. Esquire, Inc., 327 U.S. 146 (1946).

28. Compare Brooks v. Dewar, 313 U.S. 354 (1941), with *Ex parte* Endo, 323 U.S. 283 (1944).

29. Hegeman Farms Corp. v. Baldwin, 293 U.S. 163 (1934). But cf. Smith v. Cahoon, 283 U.S. 553 (1931).

30. Schneider v. State (Town of Irvington), 308 U.S. 147, 158-59 (1939). If it be suggested that the vice in licensing of speech is the conventional one of excessive delegation of legislative power, it should be remembered that ordinarily the federal Constitution is deemed not to forbid delegation by a state legislature. Highland Farms Dairy v. Agnew, 300 U.S. 608 (1937).

31. Compare United States v. Balint, 258 U.S. 250 (1922) with Smith v. California, 361 U.S. 147 (1959).

32. Morison, *Life of Harrison Gray Otis* (1913), I, 120-21.

33. Near v. Minnesota, 283 U.S. 697 (1931).

34. Cox v. New Hampshire, 312 U.S. 569 (1941) (street procession).

35. 316 U.S. 52 (1942).

36. Oklahoma Operating Co. v. Love, 252 U.S. 331 (1920), per Brandeis, J.

37. Cf. Thomas v. Collins, 323 U.S. 516, 524 (1945). See Cox, "The Void Order and the Duty to Obey," 16 *U. of Chi. L. Rev.* 86 (1948).

38. The movie-censorship case is Times Film Corp. v. Chicago, 365 U.S. 43 (1961); the earlier New York case is Kingsley Books, Inc. v. Brown, 354 U.S. 436 (1957).

39. Thornhill v. Alabama, 310 U.S. 88 (1940).

40. United States v. L. Cohen Grocery Co., 255 U.S. 81 (1921); cf. Mahler v. Eby, 264 U.S. 32 (1924).

41. Screws v. United States, 325 U.S. 91 (1945).

42. Cox v. New Hampshire, 312 U.S. 569 (1941).

43. See note, "Due Process Requirements of Definiteness in Statutes," 62 *Harv. L. Rev.* 77 (1948).

44. Musser v. Utah, 333 U.S. 95 (1948) (remand); Winters v. New York, 333 U.S. 507 (1948) (construction by state court; held invalid nevertheless). In the *Winters* case the Court said: "The interpretation by the Court of Appeals [in this case] puts these words in the statute as definitely as if it had been so amended by the legislature." 333 U.S. at 514.

45. 340 U.S. 268 (1951).

46. 340 U.S. 315 (1951).

47. 340 U.S. 290 (1951).
48. Ibid. at 293.
49. Ibid. at 295.
50. Ibid. at 297.
51. Ibid. at 298.
52. Wuchter v. Pizzutti, 276 U.S. 13 (1928).
53. 340 U.S. at 285-86. The phrase "would outrage the religious sensibilities of others" suggests a criterion short of a provocation of breach of the peace by vile or inflammatory language, such as was found in the *Feiner* case. Perhaps the passage should be read in the light of the evidence regarding Kunz's previous performances. If the case were that of a sober-minded, soberly-spoken appeal, though spoken outdoors and outraging certain sensibilities (perhaps because of its very "rationalism"), would there be adequate ground for suppression?
54. Cf. Milk Wagon Drivers Union v. Meadowmoor Dairies, Inc., 312 U.S. 287 (1941).
55. Lord Eldon's dire forebodings in 1830 may be recalled: "What is passing is a renewal of a more frightful kind than the prospects of 1791, 2, 3, 4, and 5. The occurrences of those days, involving the Crown as well as the Houses of Parliament, by express mention, in revolutionary projects—the language 'No King'—gave a treasonable character to the proceedings of that era which enabled government to deal with it by law. That is now carefully avoided, and the proceedings of this day are therefore the more difficult to be dealt with. They are, of course, more dangerous. The sacrifice, too, of the Test Act and the passing of the Roman Catholic Emancipation Bill have established a precedent so encouraging to the present attempts at revolution under name of Reform, that he must be a very bold fool who does not tremble at what seems to be fast approaching." Letter to Lord Stowell, quoted in Trevelyan, *Lord Grey of the Reform Bill* (1920), 206.
56. Goodrich, "Does the Constitution Protect Free Speech?" 19 *Mich. L. Rev.* 487, 500 (1921), reprinted in 2 *Sel. Ess. on Const. Law* 1068, 1078-79 (1938).
57. Kovacs v. Cooper, 336 U.S. 77 (1949) (concurring).
58. Santayana, "Reason in Science," in *The Life of Reason* (rev. ed., 1955), 401-02.

59. Acton, *A Lecture on the Study of History* (1905), 73.

60. Palko v. Connecticut, 302 U.S. 319, 327 (1937).

61. Dissenting in Abrams v. United States, 250 U.S. 616 (1919).

62. Dissenting in United States *ex rel.* Milwaukee Social Democratic Pub. Co. v. Burleson, 255 U.S. 407 (1921).

63. See Meiklejohn, *Free Speech* (1948), 26-27: "When men govern themselves, it is they—and no one else—who must pass judgment upon unwisdom and unfairness and danger. And that means that unwise ideas must have a hearing as well as wise ones, unfair as well as fair, dangerous as well as safe, un-American as well as American. Just so far as, at any point, the citizens who are to decide an issue are denied acquaintance with information or opinion or doubt or disbelief or criticism which is relevant to that issue, just so far the result must be ill-considered, ill-balanced planning for the general good. *It is that mutilation of the thinking process of the community against which the First Amendment to the Constitution is directed.* The principle of the freedom of speech springs from the necessities of the program of self-government. It is not a Law of Nature or of Reason in the abstract. It is a deduction from the basic American agreement that public issues shall be decided by universal suffrage." (Italics in original.)

This is not to forget how large a part is taken by the irrational in our acts and decisions. But this reminder hardly justifies committing control to those whose irrationality may be more fatal. There is always the haunting question, *Quis custodes custodiet?* Moreover, even those who find irrationality most pervasive do not regard it as all-inclusive; the psychoanalyst relies on his own rationality and even on that of his patient.

64. Martin v. Struthers, 319 U.S. 141 (1943); cf. Breard v. Alexandria, 341 U.S. 622 (1951).

65. Niebuhr, *The Children of Light and the Children of Darkness* (1953), 74.

66. *The Pilot* (Boston, Mass.), June 7, 1952.

67. See Miller, *Roger Williams* (1953).

68. Beauharnais v. Illinois, 343 U.S. 250 (1952).

69. L. Hand, "The Contribution of an Independent Judiciary to Civilization," in *The Supreme Judicial Court of Massachusetts 1692-1942* (Mass. Bar Ass'n, 1942), 59,66. And

see Curtis, "Due, and Democratic, Process of Law," 1944 *Wis. L. Rev.* 39.

70. *Ex parte* Endo, 323 U.S. 283 (1944); see *New York Times*, Dec. 18, 1944, p. 1, col. 2.

71. Hall v. United States, 168 F.2d 161 (D.C. Cir. 1948); People v. Roxborough, 307 Mich. 575 (1943), *cert. denied*, 323 U.S. 749 (1944); see 2 *Vand. L. Rev.* 111 (1948); 48 *Col. L. Rev.* 953 (1948); 61 *Harv. L. Rev.* 1455 (1948); Reppy, *Civil Rights in the United States* (1951), 180.

72. See Powell, "Judicial Protection of Civil Rights," 29 *Iowa L. Rev.* 383, 389-90 (1944).

73. 307 U.S. 496 (1939).

74. The ordinance, adopted July 6, 1939, designated certain public places, permits to speak at which could be applied for four days in advance and were to be granted unless a prior applicant had pre-empted the time and place, in which event another of the designated places would be offered. See also 36 *Code Fed. Regs.* §§3.19-3.21 (1949), giving priority to those applicants for permits to speak in public parks in the national capital who seek to answer other scheduled speakers.

75. See *Natl. Inst. Mun. L. Officers*, Rep. No. 123 (1948) (municipal control of noise); ibid., Rep. No. 124 (1948) (comic books); cf. ibid., Rep. No. 118 (1947) (peddlers, solicitors, and itinerant merchants).

76. Compare Kovacs v. Cooper, 336 U.S. 77 (1949), with Saia v. New York, 334 U.S. 558 (1948).

77. Compare Watchtower Bible & Tract Soc. v. Los Angeles County, 181 F.2d 739 (9th Cir. 1950), with Murdock v. Pennsylvania, 319 U.S. 105 (1943).

78. See Martin v. City of Struthers, 319 U.S. 141, 148 (1943) (making reference to a draft ordinance proposed by the National Institute of Municipal Law Officers).

## IV. UMPIRING THE FEDERAL SYSTEM

1. Constitution of the French Republic, Art. 91; Constitution of Switzerland, Art. 113; Fundamental Law of Yugoslavia, Arts. 16, 34(6).

2. Madison's proposal was, in fact, broader. He addressed it to the motion of Charles Pinckney, made in the Convention on June 8, 1787, that the national legislature be given the power "of negating all laws to be passed by the State legislatures which they may judge improper." *Documents Illustrative*

*of the Formation of the Union of the American States* (1927), 758. Supporting the motion, Madison "confesses it is not without its difficulties on many accounts—some may be removed, others modified, and some are unavoidable. May not this power be vested in the senatorial branch? they will probably be always sitting" (ibid., p. 759). An earlier version of Pinckney's motion, providing for a negative by two thirds of the legislature on all state laws "interfering . . . with the general interests and harmony of the Union," was opposed by Madison as being imperfectly drawn (ibid., p. 604).

3. *Ex parte* McCardle, 7 Wall. 506 (U.S. 1868).

4. See Hart, "The Power of Congress to Limit the Jurisdiction of Federal Courts: An Exercise in Dialectic," 66 *Harv. L. Rev.* 1362 (1953), reprinted in Hart and Wechsler, *The Federal Courts and the Federal System* (1953), 312-39.

5. *In re* Rahrer, 140 U.S. 545 (1891); Pennsylvania v. Wheeling and Belmont Bridge Co., 18 How. 421 (U.S. 1855); see note, "Change in Constitutional Doctrine Through Legislation," 63 *Harv. L. Rev.* 861 (1950).

6. See Helvering v. Gerhardt, 304 U.S. 405, 411 n. 1 (1938).

7. 67 Stat. 29 (1953), 43 U.S.C.A. §1301 et seq. (Supp. 1953); United States v. Texas, 339 U.S. 707 (1950); United States v. California, 332 U.S. 19 (1947); Rhode Island v. Louisiana, *motion to file bill of complaint denied,* 347 U.S. 272 (1954).

8. Steward Mach. Co. v. Davis, 301 U.S. 548 (1937); Florida v. Mellon, 273 U.S. 12 (1927); Duke Power Co. v. Greenwood County, 91 F.2d 665 (4th Cir. 1937), *aff'd,* 302 U.S. 485 (1938).

9. See Wheare, *Federal Government* (2d ed., 1951), 114-25; Bailey, "Fifty Years of the Australian Constitution," 25 *Aust. L. J.* 314, 323-25 (1951); Scott, "Centralization and Decentralization in Canadian Federalism," 29 *Can. B. Rev.* 1095, 1120 (1951). See also, for Australia, Brown, "Some Aspects of Federal-State Financial Relations," in *Federalism: An Australian Jubilee Study* (Sawer, ed., 1952), 49; for Canada, Mackintosh, "Federal Finance," ibid. at 80.

10. Loewenstein, "Reflections on the Value of Constitutions in Our Revolutionary Age," in *Constitutions and Constitutional Trends Since World War II* (Zurcher, ed., 1951), 191, 211.

11. Hood & Sons v. DuMond, 336 U.S. 525 (1949); Pennsylvania v. West Virginia, 262 U.S. 553 (1923); cf. Hudson County Water Co. v. McCarter, 209 U.S. 349 (1908); Geer v. Connecticut, 161 U.S. 519 (1896); Smith, *The Power Policy of Maine* (1951).

12. Loewenstein, op. cit., at 211-12.

13. 49 Stat. 31 (1935), 15 U.S.C. § 715(b) (1946).

14. Parker v. Brown, 317 U.S. 341 (1943); Griswold v. President of the United States, 82 F.2d 922 (5th Cir. 1936).

15. Dred Scott v. Sandford, 19 How. 393 (U.S. 1857).

16. 109 U.S. 3 (1883).

17. U.S. Const., Amend. XIV, § 5.

18. Smith v. Allwright, 321 U.S. 649 (1944); Marsh v. Alabama, 326 U.S. 501 (1946); Shelley v. Kraemer, 334 U.S. 1 (1948); Barrows v. Jackson, 346 U.S. 249 (1953).

19. Pollock v. Farmers' Loan & Trust Co., 157 U.S. 429, 554 (1895).

20. Hammer v. Dagenhart, 247 U.S. 251 (1918). For a list of constitutional amendments submitted by Congress to the states but not adopted, see H. R. Doc. No. 211, 83d Cong., 1st Sess. (1953).

21. Compare United States v. E. C. Knight Co., 156 U.S. 1 (1894), with Swift & Co. v. United States, 196 U.S. 375 (1905), Northern Securities Co. v. United States, 193 U.S. 197 (1904), and Addyston Pipe & Steel Co. v. United States, 175 U.S. 211 (1899).

22. Compare Local 167 v. United States, 291 U.S. 293 (1934), with A.L.A. Schechter Poultry Corp. v. United States, 295 U.S. 495 (1935); Coronado Coal Co. v. U.M.W., 268 U.S. 295 (1925), with Carter v. Carter Coal Co., 298 U.S. 238 (1936); New York Cent. Securities Corp. v. United States, 287 U.S. 12 (1932), with Railroad Retirement Bd. v. Alton RR., 295 U.S. 330 (1935).

23. 135 U.S. 100, 125 (1890).

24. 37 Stat. 699 (1913), 27 U.S.C. § 122 (1946).

25. See Clark Distilling Co. v. Western Md. Ry., 242 U.S. 311, 325 (1917).

26. See Eliot, "The Social Security Bill 25 Years After," *Atlantic Monthly* (Aug. 1960), p. 72.

27. Testa v. Katt, 330 U.S. 386 (1947).

28. West Virginia *ex rel.* Dyer v. Sims, 341 U.S. 22 (1951).

29. Brown v. Maryland, 12 Wheat. 419 (U.S. 1827).

30. Baldwin v. G. A. F. Seelig, Inc., 294 U.S. 511 (1935); Crossman v. Lurman, 192 U.S. 189 (1904).

31. Dean Milk Co. v. City of Madison, 340 U.S. 349 (1951).

32. Hammer v. Dagenhart, 247 U.S. 251 (1918), *overruled,* United States v. Darby, 312 U.S. 100 (1941); cf. Leisy v. Hardin, 135 U.S. 100 (1890).

33. Baldwin v. G. A. F. Seelig, Inc., 294 U.S. 511 (1935).

34. Henneford v. Silas Mason Co., 300 U.S. 577 (1937). Not all use-tax statutes grant a credit for out-of-state sales taxes. See Maxwell, *The Fiscal Impact of Federalism in the United States* (1946), 301. It has been suggested that this failure is not fatal, since the state of delivery could employ a general use tax without any sales tax, thus avoiding even the semblance of discrimination, inasmuch as there would be no deduction for sales taxes anywhere. See Powell, "New Light on Gross Receipts Taxes," 53 *Harv. L. Rev.* 909, 930-31 (1940). The problem is minimized if the state of origin cannot in any event levy a sales tax on an interstate sale. Adams Mfg. Co. v. Storen, 304 U.S. 307 (1938).

35. Sprout v. City of South Bend, 277 U.S. 163 (1928).

36. Cf. Pacific Tel. & Tel. Co. v. Tax Comm'n, 297 U.S. 403 (1936).

37. See St. Louis S. W. Ry. v. Arkansas, 235 U.S. 350, 368-69 (1914); cf. Hill v. Florida, 325 U.S. 538, 546-47 (1945) (Stone, J., dissenting).

38. See, e.g., Memphis Steam Laundry Cleaner, Inc. v. Stone, 342 U.S. 389 (1952) (alternative holding); Nippert v. Richmond, 327 U.S. 416 (1946); Robbins v. Shelby County Taxing Dist., 120 U.S. 489 (1887).

39. Johnson Oil Refining Co. v. Oklahoma, 290 U.S. 158 (1933).

40. See Minn. Laws 1945, c. 418, § 5, for a three-factor allocation formula, adopted after taxation of an entire fleet based in Minnesota was upheld in Northwest Airlines v. Minnesota, 322 U.S. 292 (1944); cf. Braniff Airways v. Nebraska State Bd., 347 U.S. 590 (1954).

41. Compare Underwood Typewriter Co. v. Chamberlain, 254 U.S. 113 (1920), with Hans Rees' Sons, Inc. v. North Carolina, 283 U.S. 123 (1931); Pullman's Palace Car Co. v. Pennsylvania, 141 U.S. 18 (1891), with Union Tank Line Co. v. Wright, 249 U.S. 275 (1919).

42. E.g., Ford Motor Co. v. Beauchamp, 308 U.S. 331 (1939) (capital stock, surplus, and undivided profits the base; gross receipts the allocation fraction); Illinois Central RR. v. Minnesota, 309 U.S. 157 (1940) (tax measured by railroads' gross earnings, imposed in lieu of all other taxes and sustained as a property tax, calculated by ratio of freight car miles within the state to total system car miles). In the latter case the taxable earnings were the net credit balance remaining after subtracting the carrier's obligations for rental of cars of other carriers on its lines from its credits for rental of its cars to other carriers on their lines. Both amounts were allocated by the car mileage ratio, and only carriers having lines within the state were taxed. The smaller the amount of trackage in the state the smaller is the amount subtracted as car rental debits and the larger the tax. If this paradoxical result is to be avoided by viewing the tax as one in lieu of a tax on cars or on credit balances for car rentals, the exemption of carriers having no lines in the state would seem to violate the equal protection clause.

43. Elsewhere I have discussed more fully the Court's reluctance to prescribe rules for choice of law. Freund, "Review and Federalism," in *Supreme Court and Supreme Law* (Cahn, ed., 1954), 86, 105-07.

44. At this point I have drawn on an earlier study, which pursues the comparison in greater detail. Freund, "A Supreme Court in a Federation: Some Lessons from Legal History," 53 *Col. L. Rev.* 597 (1953).

45. 30 Vict., c.3, § 91.

46. Attorney Gen. Can. v. Attorney Gen. Ont., [1937] A. C. 355 (P.C.); Attorney Gen. Can. v. Attorney Gen. Ont., [1937] A.C. 326 (P.C.); Attorney Gen. Brit. Colum. v. Attorney Gen. Can., [1937] A.C. 377 (P.C.).

47. Attorney Gen. Brit. Colum. v. Attorney Gen. Can., [1937] A.C. 391 (P.C.); Attorney Gen. Ont. v. Attorney Gen. Can., [1937] A.C. 405 (P.C.).

48. James v. South Australia, 40 C. L. R. 1 (Aust. 1927); James v. Cowan, [1932] A.C. 542 (P.C.); James v. Commonwealth, [1936] A.C. 578 (P.C.). Lord Wright, who participated in the decision of *James v. Commonwealth* in the Privy Council, later published a remarkable *mea culpa*, acknowledging that Section 92 should be regarded as simply a prohibition on interstate fiscal barriers, in his suggestive phrase a *laissez-*

*passer* and not a *laissez-faire* clause. Wright, "Section 92—A Problem Piece," 1 *Sydney L. Rev.* 145, 159 (1954).

49. Commonwealth v. Bank of New South Wales, [1950] A.C. 235 (P.C. 1949), *affirming* 76 C. L. R. 1 (Aust. 1948).

50. Chafee, "Charles Evans Hughes," 93 *Proc. Am. Philos. Soc'y* (1949), 267, 272.

51. See Freund, op. cit., n. 44, above, at 613 n. 64.

52. Dewey, *Reconstruction in Philosophy* (enlarged ed. 1948), 188-89, 198-99.

53. Neumann, "The Social Sciences," in *The Cultural Migration: The European Scholar in America* (Crawford, ed., 1953), 19.

54. Hartz, "The Whig Tradition in America and Europe," 46 *Am. Pol. Sci. Rev.* 989, 997 n. 10 (1952).

55. Tillich, "The Conquest of Theological Provincialism," in op. cit. n. 53, above, at 138, 145-46.

56. Compare the observation of Professor Goodhart: "In time legal thinking tends to influence lay thinking, and I believe that the average Englishman's dislike and distrust of rumour and scandal in political and social life is due in part to the fact that he has been taught that hearsay evidence is not to be believed." Goodhart, *English Law and the Moral Law* (1953), 136.

## V. PORTRAIT OF A LIBERAL JUDGE: MR. JUSTICE BRANDEIS

1. Pollock v. Farmers' Loan & Trust Co., 158 U.S. 601, 695 (1895).

2. Liverpool, New York & Philadelphia SS. Co. v. Commissioners of Emigration, 113 U.S. 33, 39 (1885).

3. Chicago, M. & St. P. Ry. v. Minnesota, 134 U.S. 418 (1890) (dissent); Wabash, St. L. & P. Ry. v. Illinois, 118 U.S. 557 (1886) (dissent). See Fairman, "The Education of a Justice," 1 *Stanford L. Rev.* 217, 218-19 (1949). Compare Bradley's earlier views in Davidson v. New Orleans, 96 U.S. 97, 107 (1878).

4. Introduction to "The Sins of Legislators," in Spencer, *The Man Versus the State* (Truxton Beale, ed., Caldwell, Idaho: The Caxton Printers, Ltd., 1916. Used by special permission of the copyright owners), 241.

5. Brandeis, "The Employer and Trades Unions" (1904), and "Organized Labor and Efficiency" (1911), printed in *Business—A Profession* (1933 ed.), 13, 37.

6. "Knowledge is essential to understanding; and understanding should precede judging." Jay Burns Baking Co. v. Bryan, 264 U.S. 504, 520 (1924) (dissenting).

7. Nashville, C. & St. L. Ry. v. Walters, 294 U.S. 405 (1935). Cf. also Hammond v. Schappi Bus Line, 275 U.S. 164 (1927).

8. Carmichael v. Southern Coal Co., 301 U.S. 495 (1937).

9. A very different view of fidelity insurance was taken by the philosopher Josiah Royce. "Ours is already an age and a civilization of insurance," he observed, adding that "fidelity insurance, working in more or less indirect fashion, enables countless young men to begin life in positions of trust, and thus to find their places as people worthy of confidence in a world where they might otherwise be doomed to live only as temporary employees." Royce, *The Hope of the Great Community* (1916), 72-73. A Brandeisian end, it may be remarked, reached by un-Brandeisian means.

10. Texas & Pacific Ry. v. Pottorff, 291 U.S. 245 (1934); McNair v. Knott, 302 U.S. 369 (1937). Cf. also Lewis v. Fidelity & Deposit Co. of Maryland, 292 U.S. 559 (1934).

11. New State Ice Co. v. Liebmann, 285 U.S. 262, 309-11 (1932) (dissenting).

12. Liggett v. Lee, 288 U.S. 517, 541 (1933) (dissenting).

13. Myers v. United States, 272 U.S. 52 (1926).

14. United States v. Smith, 286 U.S. 6 (1932).

15. Ashwander v. TVA, 297 U.S. 288, 341 (1936) (concurring).

16. 304 U.S. 64 (1938).

17. Willing v. Chicago Auditorium Assn., 277 U.S. 274 (1928); Nashville, C. & St. L. Ry. v. Wallace, 288 U.S. 249 (1933).

18. Northern Pac. Ry. v. Department of Public Works, 268 U.S. 39, 44-45 (1925).

19. Oklahoma Operating Co. v. Love, 252 U.S. 331, 338 (1920).

20. St. Joseph Stock Yards Co. v. United States, 298 U.S. 38, 77 (1936) (concurring).

21. Senn v. Tile Layers Protective Union, 301 U.S. 468, 478 (1937).

22. Duplex Printing Press Co. v. Deering, 254 U.S. 443, 488 (1921) (dissenting).

23. 248 U.S. 215, 248 (1918) (dissenting).

24. 262 U.S. 553, 605 (1923) (dissenting).
25. Dahnke-Walker Milling Co. v. Bondurant, 257 U.S. 282, 293 (1921) (dissenting).
26. *Dissertationes*, Bk. III, Ch. 24, quoted in Toynbee, *Study of History*, VI, 147, n. 1 (1939). For a penetrating treatment of stoicism and advocacy, see Curtis, "A Lawyer's 'Entire' Devotion to his Client," 34 *A. B. A. J.* 805 (1948).
27. Bradford Electric Light Co. v. Clapper, 284 U.S. 221 (1931).
28. John Hancock Mutual Life Ins. Co. v. Yates, 299 U.S. 178 (1936).
29. Yarborough v. Yarborough, 290 U.S. 202 (1933).
30. 248 U.S. 215 (1918).
31. 277 U.S. 438 (1928).
32. Warren and Brandeis, "The Right to Privacy," 4 *Harv. L. Rev.* 193 (1890).
33. MS. in the Harvard Law School Library.
34. 277 U.S. at 473-74, 478.
35. Hearings before Committee on the Judiciary, U.S. Senate, 74th Cong., 1st Sess., on S. 2176, p. 10.
36. 254 U.S. 325 (1920).
37. 262 U.S. 390 (1923).
38. 276 U.S. 413 (1928).
39. 271 U.S. 142 (1926).
40. Burnet v. Coronado Oil & Gas Co., 285 U.S. 393, 406 (1932) (dissenting).
41. 304 U.S. 64 (1938).
42. Conversely, his approach to the problem of education reflected his attachment to federalism; witness his selection of the University of Louisville as an object of his bounty and solicitude. Bernard Flexner's monograph *Mr. Justice Brandeis and the University of Louisville* (1938) gives a most revealing insight into Brandeis's insistence on both vision and mastery of detail, in the context of an endeavor to enrich the life of a state. See also Freund, "Mr. Justice Brandeis: A Centennial Memoir," 70 *Harv. L. Rev.* 769 (1957).
43. Whitney v. California, 274 U.S. 357, 375 (1927).

## VI. JUDGE AND COMPANY

1. *Theaetetus* (Jowett translation).
2. "Augustus Noble Hand," 61 *Harv. L. Rev.* 573, 585.
3. 316 U.S. 455 (1942).

4. Korematsu v. United States, 323 U.S. 214 (1944).

5. Warren, *Supreme Court in United States History* (rev. ed., 1937), I, 610-11.

6. 7 How. 1 (1849).

7. *Writings and Speeches of Daniel Webster* (1903), XI, 219.

8. Norman v. Baltimore & Ohio RR., 294 U.S. 240 (1935).

9. Hughes, *The Supreme Court of the United States* (1928), 50-54.

10. Cf. Norman v. Consolidated Edison Co., 89 F.2d 619 (2d Cir., 1937).

11. E.g., Moor v. Texas & N. O. R. Co., 297 U.S. 101 (1936).

12. Muller v. Oregon, 208 U.S. 412 (1908). The opinion of the Court, upholding the law, was delivered by Mr. Justice Brewer, generally not distinguished for sympathy toward social legislation. He did, however, exhibit marked sympathy for womankind; see, e.g., *In re* Bort, 25 Kans. 308 (1881). He stands as a reminder that sentimentality in a judge is not an adequate substitute for a philosophy of government.

13. Argument in Stettler v. O'Hara, 243 U.S. 629 (1917), printed in *The Curse of Bigness: Miscellaneous Papers of Justice Brandeis* (Fraenkel, ed., 1934), 52, 65-66.

14. Carter v. Carter Coal Co., 298 U.S. 238 (1936).

15. Alabama Power Co. v. Ickes, 302 U.S. 464 (1938).

16. Tennessee Electric Power Co. v. TVA, 306 U.S. 118 (1939).

17. Ashwander v. TVA, 297 U.S. 288 (1936).

18. 90 F.2d 885 (6th Cir., 1937).

19. See n. 16, above.

20. *In re* American States Public Service Co., 12 F. Supp. 667 (D.Md. 1935).

21. *In re* Central West Public Service Co., 13 F. Supp. 239 (D.Del. 1935).

22. Transcript of Record, pp. 304-05, in Burco v. Whitworth, reported at 81 F.2d 721 (4th Cir. 1936).

23. Ibid., at 306.

24. See n. 20, above.

25. Burco v. Whitworth (see above, n. 22).

26. Burco v. Whitworth, 297 U.S. 724 (1936).

27. Landis v. North American Co., 299 U.S. 248 (1936).

28. Electric Bond & Share Co. v. SEC, 303 U.S. 419 (1938).

29. United States v. Bankers Trust Co., 294 U.S. 240 (1935).

30. Helvering v. Davis, 301 U.S. 619 (1937). The decision of the district court was rendered on January 27, 1937; that of the Circuit Court of Appeals on April 14; and that of the Supreme Court on May 24.

31. United States v. Belcher, 294 U.S. 736 (1935).

32. United States v. Darby, 312 U.S. 100 (1941); Kentucky Whip & Collar Co. v. Illinois Central RR., 299 U.S. 334 (1937).

33. United States v. Certain Lands in Louisville, 297 U.S. 726 (1936).

34. See above, p. 54.

35. James v. Dravo Contracting Co., 302 U.S. 134 (1937).

36. Helvering v. Gerhardt, 304 U.S. 405 (1938) (in which the Court's decision was more sweeping than the government's argument; see above, p. 54); Graves v. New York *ex rel.* O'Keefe, 306 U.S. 466 (1939).

37. Alabama v. King & Boozer, 314 U.S. 1 (1941).

38. United States v. Allegheny County, 322 U.S. 174, 193 (1944) (dissenting).

## VII. THE COURT AND ITS CRITICS

1. Brewer, "Government by Injunction," 15 *Nat. Corp. Rep.* 848, 849 (1898).

2. See Warren, *The Supreme Court in United States History* (1926), I, 555-56.

3. Buchanan v. Warley, 245 U.S. 60 (1917).

4. Missouri *ex rel.* Gaines v. Canada, 305 U.S. 337, 353 (1938).

5. Whitehead, *Symbolism, Its Meaning and Effect* (1927), 88.

6. See the discussion in Chapter I, above.

7. E.g., Canton RR. v. Rogan, 340 U.S. 511 (1951); Railway Express Agency v. Virginia, 358 U.S. 434 (1959); City of Detroit v. Murray Corp., 355 U.S. 489 (1958).

8. Colegrove v. Green, 328 U.S. 549 (1946); South v. Peters, 339 U.S. 276 (1950).

9. Yates v. United States, 354 U.S. 298 (1957).

10. Wiemann v. Updegraff, 344 U.S. 183 (1954).

11. Communist Party v. Subversive Activities Control Board, 351 U.S. 115 (1956).
12. Watkins v. United States, 354 U.S. 178 (1957).
13. Kent v. Dulles, 357 U.S. 116 (1958).
14. Peters v. Hobby, 359 U.S. 331 (1955); Greene v. McElroy, 360 U.S. 474 (1959).
15. Schware v. Board of Bar Examiners, 353 U.S. 232 (1957).
16. Griffin v. Illinois, 351 U.S. 12 (1956).
17. Sweezy v. New Hampshire, 354 U.S. 234 (1957). But cf. Barenblatt v. United States, 360 U.S. 109 (1959).
18. 350 U.S. 497 (1956).
19. Slochower v. Board of Education, 350 U.S. 551 (1956) (Reed, Burton, Minton, and Harlan, JJ., dissenting).
20. Beilan v. Board of Education, 357 U.S. 399 (1958); Lerner v. Casey, 357 U.S. 468 (1958) (Warren, C. J., and Black, Douglas, and Brennan, JJ., dissenting).
21. Nelson and Globe v. County of Los Angeles, 362 U.S. 1 (1960) (Black, Douglas, and Brennan, JJ., dissenting; Warren, C. J., not participating). In the case of a "permanent" employee the Court was evenly divided.
22. Griswold, "Foreword" to Supreme Court note, 74 *Harv. L. Rev.* 81 (1960).
23. Konigsberg v. State Bar, 353 U.S. 252 (1957). The decision was narrowly interpreted and qualified when the case again reached the Supreme Court. 366 U.S. 36 (1961) (Warren, C. J., Black, Douglas, and Brennan, JJ., dissenting).
24. See n. 12 and n. 17, above.
25. Griffin v. Illinois, 351 U.S. 12 (1956); Eskridge v. Washington Prison Board, 357 U.S. 214 (1958).
26. Schneider v. State, 308 U.S. 147 (1939).
27. N. A. A. C. P. v. Alabama, 357 U.S. 449 (1958).
28. Lewis Publ. Co. v. Morgan, 229 U.S. 228 (1913).
29. United States v. Harriss, 347 U.S. 612 (1954).
30. Talley v. California, 362 U.S. 60 (1960) (Clark, Frankfurter, and Whittaker, JJ., dissenting).
31. Hudson County Water Co. v. McCarter, 209 U.S. 349, 355 (1908).
32. On the "ethical" aspects of scientific thinking, see Morton White, *Toward Reunion in Philosophy* (1956), 254-58, 277-78.

# INDEX